THE JOY OF WORK

Dilbert's Guide to Finding Happiness at the Expense of Your Co-workers

SCOTT ADAMS

A HarperBusiness Book
from HarperPerennial

A hardcover edition of this book was published in 1998 by HarperBusiness, a division of HarperCollins Publishers, Inc.

Designed by Nancy Singer Olaguera

First HarperPerennial edition published 1999.

The Library of Congress has catalogued the hardcover edition as follows:
Adams, Scott, 1957–
    The joy of work : Dilbert's guide to finding happiness at the expense of your co-workers / Scott Adams. — 1st ed.
      p. cm.
    ISBN 0-88730-871-6
    1. Humor in the workplace—United States.   2. Corporate culture—United States.   3. Industrial management—Social aspects—United States.   I. Title.
HF5549.5.H85A32   1998
650.1—DC21   98-27083

ISBN 0-88730-895-3 (pbk.)

99 00 01 02 03 ❖/RRD 10 9 8 7 6 5 4 3 2

*This book is dedicated to the wonderful people
who have helped populate the Dilbert comic
and Dilbert books with their suggestions, anecdotes,
and observations. And Pam too.*

Contents

1

The Joy of Work

I cried because I did not have an office with a door,
until I met a man who had no cubicle.

—DILBERT

Maybe you've heard of something called the "open plan" office design. It's getting a lot of attention lately. Under the open plan, employees have no offices or cubicles, just desks in a large open area. Storage areas are virtually eliminated. This is not a good trend.

After your boss has taken away your door, your walls, and your storage areas, there aren't many options left for the next revolution in office design. One of the following things is likely to go next:

▶ The floor

▶ The ceiling

▶ Your happiness

I think the floor will stay, but only because your company would have to dig a huge hole all the way to the other side of the earth to get rid of it. As you can imagine, a huge hole through the earth would represent a serious threat to office productivity. Depending on your global location, the other side of the world might have hordes of refugees who would run through the hole, take one look at your office, scream in horror, and run back home. It's hard enough to concentrate while your co-workers are yammering, but if you add hordes of screaming refugees coming out of a hole, things would only get worse. And don't get me started about the problems with molten lava, or the fact that if you puncture the earth, all the gravity would escape.

Your company won't remove your ceiling. You need the ceiling to keep the people who are on higher floors from falling on your head. The only exception is the people on the top floor of your building, i.e., the ones who ordered your cubicle to be taken away. They'll keep their ceilings too, because all of the discomforts that make regular employees *more* productive are exactly the kinds of things that make senior executives *less* productive. No one knows why.

I think the next wave of office design will focus on eliminating the only remaining obstacle to office productivity: your happiness. Happiness isn't a physical thing, like walls and doors. But it's closely related. Managers know that if they can eliminate all traces of happiness, the employees won't be so picky about their physical surroundings. Once you're hopelessly unhappy, you won't bother to complain if your boss rolls you up in a tight ball and crams you into a cardboard box.

As soon as I noticed this disturbing threat to workplace happiness, I did some investigative work and discovered it wasn't confined to the issue of office design. Companies were making a direct frontal assault on employee happiness in every possible way! I knew there was only one thing that could stop the horror.

It was time for another Dilbert book.

It might sound corny, but I felt an obligation to society. People told me it was time for me to "give something back to the community." This scared me until I realized that no one knows I furnished my house with street signs and park benches. So I interpreted the "give back to the community" message as a plea for me to write this book and then charge the community to read it.

In the first part of this book I will tell you how to find happiness at the expense of your co-workers, managers, customers, and—best of all—those lazy stockholders. The second part of the book teaches you my top-secret methods for mining humor out of ordinary situations, thus making it easier to mock the people around you. The third part of the book is made entirely of invisible pages. If the book seems heavier than it looks, that's why.

► HAPPINESS CREATES MONEY

In recent years, large companies revived an economic theory that had been out of fashion for hundreds of years. It goes something like this:

Economic Theory of the Nineties

Anything that makes employees unhappy makes the
stock price go up.

Economics is a murky field, so when you find something that's easy to understand, you tend to latch on to it. You couldn't fault managers for reaching the conclusion that employee happiness and stock prices are inversely related. The evidence was impossible to ignore.

Things That Make Employees Unhappy	Result
Downsizing	Stock goes up
Reduced benefits	Stock goes up
Unpaid overtime	Stock goes up
Doubling the workload	Stock goes up

The old saying about capitalism was, "A rising tide lifts all boats." If you own a boat, that's an inspirational thought. But if you work in a cubicle, rising water means one of your brilliant co-workers tried to flush the company newsletter down the toilet. Obviously, one theory does not fit all people. The economic theory that is good for stockholders is not necessarily the exact same one that is good for employees. You need your own economic theory—one that puts value on the things that matter most to you: happiness and money.

I'm highly qualified to create this new theory of economics for employees because I'm more than just a comic strip writer. *I was an actual economics major in college.* I didn't master every little nuance about economics, but I did get a good grasp of the major concepts, which I will summarize here so you don't need to become educated:

EVERYTHING I LEARNED FROM ECONOMICS CLASSES

▶ Something about supply and demand

▶ Boredom can't kill you, but you might wish it could

Those economic insights won't solve all of your problems right away, but it's a strong foundation upon which we can build.

Let's start by examining our economic assumptions. The strong economy of recent years has turned the old assumptions upside down. In the past, it was always true that if you had money—even a little bit—you could buy a lot more happiness.

Two hundred years ago, for example, a few extra dollars meant the difference between sleeping cozily indoors versus shivering under a pile of leaves until you were eaten by coyotes. Thanks to a robust economy, not to mention confusing new IRA options, life has vastly improved, coyote-wise. Money is no longer the difference between life and death for most white-collar workers. If you have a reasonable job, money can't buy nearly as much happiness as it used to. The economists would express it this way:

happiness of driving[Porsche – Hyundai] <

happiness[(not eaten by coyote) – (eaten by coyote)]

Historically, your happiness was so closely related to money that you and your employer had compatible goals. Your company wanted to make money, and you were glad to help, because it improved your odds of prying some of it out of their greedy, clenched fists. That symbiotic situation persisted for decades, until the nineties, when managers realized it was more profitable to screw their employees than to sell more products. Businesses used the "screw the employees" economic strategy to rack up incredible profits. Employees were left without a viable economic strategy of their own. Until now.

I have developed a new theory of economics for employees. According to my theory, employees should stop trying to make money directly (by doing good work) and concentrate on making themselves happy (using the powerful methods in this book). The money will follow. I'll explain how.

New Economic Theory for Employees

Happiness Creates Money

Technically, a theory is not a theory until someone tries to explain why it works. I believe there are several reasons why happy people make more money. The first reason has to do with risk.

RISK

In business, whenever you take higher risks, you improve your chances of getting rich, unless you choose a dead-end career, like skunk juggler, or prison guard, or journalist. In those cases, extra risk won't help one bit. But, in general, risk-takers make more money.

If you get your happiness from enough different sources, you aren't bothered too much if one risk goes bad. For the happy person, it's no big deal to take career chances that could result in humiliation, embarrassment, and job loss. Those things are all temporary in nature and won't have much impact on the person who has a well-diversified portfolio of happiness.

Under bad economic conditions, my theory that happiness creates money doesn't hold. The risks are too high. At the first sign of unauthorized mirth, you'll be downsized. From a manager's perspective, it's always easiest to fire the employee who isn't already an emotional basket case. Being happy during bad economic times is like painting a target on your back. If you're smart, you'll avoid any outward displays of happiness when the economy is bad.

Luckily, we aren't in bad economic times. In a booming economy you can take some extra happiness-related risks at work. Your boss won't want to fire you because he'll have to pay more money for your replacement—if he can even find one. And the replacement might be an even bigger troublemaker than you are. The balance of power has changed. Now it's even safe to make insulting jokes at the expense of your boss. You'll be amazed at how much whimsical insolence your boss is willing to tolerate. Take full advantage of this situation while it lasts.

In the unlikely event that you do get fired, you'll probably end up happy that it happened. There isn't much of a stigma to getting fired anymore, because so many people have been downsized through no fault of their own. In a few short years, getting fired has gone from a horrific experience to, arguably, an excellent way to enjoy some time off and then advance your career. If you're working in a company that gives money to people when they're fired, that's the best of all worlds. Take the money and find yourself a higher-paying job at a company that has a sense of humor.

► HAPPY PEOPLE GET BETTER JOBS

When the economy is slow, all the best jobs are taken by people with great hair. The rest of us are forced to scramble for the crumbs. But in the current robust economy, there aren't enough pretty-haired people to fill the best jobs. In good economic times, happiness—specifically a good sense of humor—can give you an edge. Humor is a tie-breaker for people whose hair has limited career potential. A good sense of humor will allow you to rise above the humorless masses and get the high-paying job you know you don't deserve.

Don't worry so much about your actual qualifications for a higher-paying job. The next employer who interviews you isn't likely to be any better at spotting your defects than your last employer was. Most managers are exceedingly bad at making hiring decisions. If you gave Charles Manson a shave and combed his bangs over the swastika on his forehead, he could get hired as the CEO of Apple Computers tomorrow. This might sound like an exaggeration, but remember: The one thing that all workplace violence has in common is that the person doing the violence got hired by a manager who didn't see the early warning signs. You have to wonder how those job interviews went:

Manager: Your résumé says your hobbies include setting fire to helpless woodland creatures. Tell me about that.

Applicant: Stop badgering me. I'm warning you.

Manager: Did you have a salary range in mind?

Applicant: There's a salary?

Managers know full well that they can't tell the difference between one job candidate and the next. All things being equal, hairwise, a hiring manager will choose the job candidate who is the most entertaining. Later in this book I'll teach you my secret formula for creating humor. That's all the training you'll need to impress your next job interviewer and land a cool job that you previously thought was out of reach, e.g.,

- ► Space shuttle pilot

- ► Designer of nuclear-tipped warheads

- ► Heart-transplant surgeon

Don't worry that you're not qualified for those positions. No one is qualified for any job on the first day. And most jobs are not as complicated as you would think. For example, it *sounds* like it would be hard to drive the space shuttle. But do you think NASA would spend a bizillion dollars building a spacecraft and then make the mistake of giving it a stick shift? The shuttle probably flies itself. It goes up, it flies in circles, it lands. They're not asking anyone to navigate through an asteroid field and bomb a Death Star. The pilots probably spend the entire time in the cockpit making rocket noises with their lips and trying to resist the temptation to touch buttons. I'll bet the shuttle pilots could trade places with the experimental gerbils in the back and you'd get the same mission results.

It sounds like it would be hard to design nuclear-tipped warheads. It probably would be hard if you cared whether your warheads actually explode. But if you think about it, the only time anyone will find out if you did a good job is when the air is filled with incoming nukes from the other side. I doubt you'll be worried about your next raise. And if that day never comes, no one will be the wiser that the detonation mechanisms for your nuclear warheads are actually the insides of old clock radios.

As for heart-transplant surgery, no one will know you didn't study medicine if you stick to highly experimental methods that are expected to fail anyway. While other surgeons are putting human hearts in human patients, you could be the doctor experimenting with the controversial procedure of putting artichoke hearts in pigs. No one will expect a high success rate there, and when the patient dies, you've got most of the fixings for a luau.

▶ BEING FUNNY MAKES YOU LOOK SMART

It's an established fact that a good sense of humor is highly correlated with genius. I say this partly because I'm in the midst of writing a humor book and partly because when you say "it's an established fact" no one ever checks to see if it really is. Whether it's true or not makes no difference. All that matters is that people *think* humor is correlated with genius. Therefore, the more humor you bring to work, the smarter you look. In the business world, a false image of intelligence is a valuable asset for your career. In fact, fake intelligence is even more useful than real intelligence. People who are genuinely smart get peevish during meetings because they have the misfortune to understand what's going on. But if you're only *pretending* to be smart, the pay is the same as if you *actually* are smart, and almost nothing can ruin your day.

Humor is the easiest and safest way to pretend you are smart. If you try to demonstrate your brilliance by, for example, shouting the solutions to complex math problems, people will think you're a dork.

But if you crack jokes all day, you'll look like a brilliant employee who is simply too modest to perform any conspicuous acts of competence on the job. As a funny employee, you'll be able to bungle one project after another without drawing suspicion that the problem is you.

► GIVING YOURSELF A STEALTH RAISE

The only reason your company pays you is because you'd rather be doing something else. The entire economic system depends on the fact that people are willing to do unpleasant things in return for money. The more hideous the task, the more money you get. Take brain surgery, for example. That job pays very well, but you have to touch people's brains all day. I don't know about you, but I'm sufficiently frightened by what comes out of people's mouths; I sure don't want to get my fingers any closer to the source. And although I haven't tried it, I'm certain I wouldn't enjoy any activity that involves handsaws and human skulls. To me, that's unpleasant.

In a sense, there's a rough equivalence between money and unpleasantness. If you accept more unpleasantness, you can make more money. Likewise, you can often decrease the unpleasantness in your life by spending money to make it go away.

$$(more\ money) = (less\ unpleasantness)$$

If you can decrease the unpleasantness that you experience at work, without taking a cut in pay, it's almost the same as giving yourself a raise. It's like a stealth raise, because your boss might not even notice. The best way to reduce your total daily exposure to unpleasantness is to crowd it out with liberal doses of happiness. This book will give you lots of strategies for adding happiness to your workday, leaving fewer hours for listening to your boss, or sawing skulls, or whatever it is that you do.

2

Managing Your Boss

Nothing is more critical to your happiness than learning to manage your boss. The alternative can be a disaster. If your boss tries to turn the tables and manage you, the next thing you know, you'll be doing moronic tasks in return for money.

In this chapter you will learn a number of boss-managing strategies that have been proven in the field. Your choice of strategy will depend on what type of boss you have. Use this grid to identify your boss.

▶ BOSS TYPES

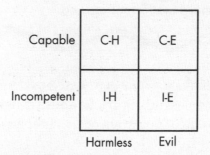

	Harmless	Evil
Capable	C-H	C-E
Incompetent	I-H	I-E

If your boss falls into the Incompetent-Evil (I-E) quadrant, select the strategies that help you stay away from him. As a rule, it's a good idea to stay away from anything in life that has "evil" built right into the description. But it's especially true where a boss is involved. When evil is combined with incompetence, it becomes more unpredictable. Your only defense is distance. Pick the strategy that puts you far out of harm's way, as this gentleman did by leaving the company.

From: [name withheld]
To: scottadams@aol.com

Each day my ex-co-workers and I picked a new word of the day. On the day I resigned, the word was "acephalous." Acephalous means "headless or lacking a clearly defined head" or "having no leader."

Later that day I was asked by the president why I had decided to leave the company. I explained to him that we had differing management styles and that, "I cannot bring myself to agree with your acephalous management practices."

He replied, "That's because you don't have the experience I do in these matters." I agreed.

In the unlikely event that your boss is in the rare category of Capable-Harmless (C-H), try to upward-delegate as much of your work as possible. You want your company to be in the hands of capable people. That way your employer can make enough money to pay people like you for doing things like reading this book.

From: [name withheld]
To: scottadams@aol.com

After experimenting with many methods, I have found that the best method of managing my boss is to keep a fresh supply of sweets in the candy jar on my desk. First, this ploy guarantees that he'll drop by my office a minimum of three times a day—and these visits make great opportunities to practice my "upward delegation" skills. Second, it ensures that my boss is on a permanent sugar high—which typically makes it easier to get positive responses from him on many crucial issues like budget approvals, extra time off, etc.

If your boss is an Incompetent-Harmless (I-H) type, you might want to keep him nearby just for the entertainment value. Several of the strategies below will help you get the most out an I-H boss.

From: [name withheld]
To: scottadams@aol.com

I work in a cube farm with about 30 feet between the rows, which is exactly the required distance for a game of "Boss Pong." To start the game you wait until the "ball" (clueless management drone) walks through, then call him over.

Now it's the opposite side's turn to divert him over to their side, otherwise we score a point.

The "ball" usually tires of the game after several volleys and won't play for a few days. With practice you will be able to play games with multiple "balls." We have had as many as four in play with seven volleys.

If your boss is a Capable-Evil (C-E) type, use the strategies that encourage him to focus on your co-workers. Hiding won't help you manage a C-E boss. He's too smart for that. Your only hope is to redirect his evil intentions where they won't hurt you. This is essentially the same strategy you use if you are being chased by a monster, i.e., throwing someone else in the path so you can get away. Here's how one employee trained his boss to focus elsewhere.

From: [name withheld]
To: scottadams@aol.com

To minimize all contacts with my boss I pretend to be even more boring than I really am. When he stops by, I'll talk about weather or science fiction stories I've read. If he asks how I'm doing, I'll start talking about a little flu I had two weeks ago, or some other nonsense, and it all ends very quickly. I've managed to manage my boss out of my life while still getting paid.

▶ BOSS-MANAGING STRATEGIES

STRATEGY 1: INDUCE TENSION

Always be prepared to unload a batch of gnarled, rotting "issues" on your boss anytime he gets within a hundred yards. Before he opens his mouth, say, "I was just looking for you!" and then proceed to describe a business problem that is as unsolvable as it is demoralizing. Here are some examples of the types of issues to unload on your boss:

Issues for Your Boss

"The Federal Trade Commission just asked for all our documents. Don't worry, we've covered the furniture with gasoline and we're waiting for your signal."

"The bad news is that there's a deadly bacteria in our air-conditioning system. The good news is that we think the asbestos in the ceiling will kill it."

"There was a mix-up in the graphics department. The logo on your new product seems to be a dead goat. At the national press conference today, try to cover it with your thumb."

If your boss has any sort of central nervous system at all, his body will suddenly stiffen and his blood pressure will rise until his eyeballs look like a freeway map. He might spontaneously grow a hunch on his back right there in front of you. Offer no proposed solutions to the "issues." Look to your boss for the answer. Act miffed if he draws a blank. The miffed expression helps convey the message that you're disappointed in his leadership. Your goal is to make every interaction a life-draining, painful experience (for him), but not in a way that could get you fired. After all, it's your job to raise issues. There's nothing wrong with that.

In time, your boss will experience something like a mild panic attack whenever he thinks of you. This will reduce his desire to give you new assignments, while at the same time making you seem like someone who cares about the big picture. Consistency is the key to this strategy. If you keep it up, eventually your boss will lose any interest in knowing what you do all day. That frees up lots of time for your important hobbies, such as napping and snacking.

STRATEGY 2: YOUR BOSS'S BOSS

If possible, try to carpool with your boss's boss. Move to a new town if you have to. It's worth it. Mention your carpooling situation to your boss often, while referring to your boss's boss by an affectionate nickname that you make up, such as Spanky or Thumper. If your boss asks you to do something you don't want to do, agree to do it, then shake your head and mumble, "Spanky will get a good laugh over this."

Alternately, join the same church as your boss's boss, even if it means switching religions. (You can always switch back after you retire, usually with no penalty in the afterlife.) While your boss might try to stop you from carpooling—by switching your work hours, for example—he wouldn't dare try to talk you out of your religion. Especially if it's the same religion as his boss's.

Whatever your method, don't get to your boss's boss during work hours. That's insubordination any way you slice it.

STRATEGY 3: WITHHOLD INFORMATION

It's safe to give your boss "issues," but never give your boss any other information about a project. If you give him actual information, he'll try to make a decision. If that doesn't worry you, consider that your boss allows you to keep your job, and you're reading a book about how to screw him. Obviously your boss's judgment isn't good. To compound matters, decisions made by your boss usually result in more work for you.

If your boss insists on status reports, use the power of "big words" to obscure any meaningful content. Here's a status report that you can use for just about any situation:

> The project initiatives are performing according to
> the variable methodology described at our strategic
> directional pre-consensus framework.

Another approach is to pretend you are even more frustrated than your boss with the fact that the information isn't available. This e-mail explains it best.

From: [name withheld]
To: scottadams@aol.com

Whenever a question is posed to me in a meeting, I carefully weigh whether or not the person asking will understand the full implications of an honest answer. When I decide that the real answer would not be the most appropriate response for this person, I simply bang my fist on the table and declare, "That's what I want to know!" This has been especially effective in meetings when the pressure is on me to provide information that is not at hand.

By varying the inflection in your voice and really emphasizing different words, this phrase can serve you well:

1 — **THAT's** what I want to know!

2 — That's what *I* want to know!

If you are forced to give regular status reports during staff meetings, make sure your report is laden with excruciating detail about trivial elements of your job. Be passionate about these details, so your boss is dissuaded from interrupting you. Eventually your boss will learn to schedule shorter meetings so there isn't time for people like you to give status reports.

An effective way to withhold information is to deluge your boss with so much information that the real messages get lost or ignored. You can train your boss to never read an e-mail message from you again. Once you've established that reflex in your boss, you have complete deniability if accused later of not keeping him informed. Just look him straight in the eye, act exasperated, and say, "I sent you four e-mail messages on that topic. Aren't you reading them?"

The degree of information you withhold should be directly proportional to the level of management you're trying to manage.

The higher up the chain, the more damage they can do with less information. A good rule of thumb is that information should be completely scrubbed of all content if it will be viewed by a manager who is two levels or more above you.

STRATEGY 4: PROXIMITY AVOIDANCE

There is a direct correlation between your boss's proximity and your happiness. I will express the relationship here in movie terms.

Boss's Proximity	Your Mood
In your cubicle	. . . like Sigourney Weaver in *Alien*.
In his own office	. . . like E.T. hiding in a closet.

Boss's Proximity	Your Mood
Another building	. . . like Dorothy after the flying monkeys leave.
Out of town	. . . like Richard Dreyfus in *Jaws,* when the water is too quiet.
Iraqi prison	. . . like Jimmy Stewart in *It's a Wonderful Life*.

One approach to the proximity problem is to stop going to the office and see how long it takes anyone to notice. But this is only a short-term solution, because if it works, your co-workers will stay home too. Soon your company will fail. At that point your boss might notice that his checks stop coming. That's when your little plot will unravel. A more clever approach is to go to work every day but find ways to get your boss out of the office, preferably to a despotic nation that considers itself at war with yours.

Scan trade journals for advertisements about faraway conferences. Pick conferences that have important-sounding words in the name, like Global, or Tech, or Symposium. Then plead with your boss to let *you* attend. This is a trick, because you have no intention of attending. Most bosses will take the bait and tell you that conferences of that sort are intended for higher-level managers. Why else would it have "Global" in the name? Curse softly and shuffle away. Repeat.

STRATEGY 5: DECOYS

Your boss has a deep psychological need to feel that he has "helped." Unfortunately, the quantity of "help" that your boss provides will have no correlation to his abilities or your needs.

Every employee who interacts with the boss will get a little dollop of "help" no matter how much is needed. That's why you need decoys.

Before making any proposal to your boss, insert some decoy steps. The decoys are elements of your plan that you don't actually intend to do. Make sure the decoys are the most obvious parts of the plan—ones that cannot be missed. Your first slide might read this way:

Phase One

- Research the market for new toys
- Design toy
- **Assassinate the president of Chile**
- Produce toy

Your boss will notice that the third bullet "doesn't fit." He'll demand that you get rid of that step. Put up some resistance (just for show) and then reluctantly agree. Ask for more money in your budget to make that change. This will satisfy your boss's need to "help." Later, confide in your boss that although you doubted him at the time, it turned out to be a good decision to cancel the hit.

STRATEGY 6: DO BAD WORK IN IMPORTANT-SOUNDING FIELDS

Don't make the mistake of working extra hard in hopes of getting the biggest raise in your department. The difference between performing at "exceeds expectations" levels versus "meets expectations" is likely to be about 2 percent per year. Mathematically speaking, in the long run you're much better off doing a lousy job at something that looks good on a résumé as opposed to doing a superb job at something that sounds dull. If your boss assigns you to something that won't help your résumé, just ignore him and dive into a job that looks good on paper, no matter how unqualified you are. Your boss won't like it one bit, but remind him to be nice because someday he might be working for you, and he'd better not burn any bridges.

You're probably not planning to stay with your current company forever, so it doesn't really matter how often you blow things. If you don't quit after a few years, you'll be downsized in the next corporate merger anyway. So building a track record of success is a silly strategy for your career.

When you interview at the new company, they won't ask your current employer for a reference, because that would reveal your disloyalty to them and get you in trouble. The only thing the new company can find out is your job "experience," not your competence. Experience is reflected in the job titles you held, without regard to your massive disloyalty, sloth, and fiduciary misconduct. If you've spent five years designing advanced aircraft engines, it doesn't matter that you only designed one engine and it leveled a nearby logging town. That information doesn't travel with you. Only the good news does: You designed advanced aircraft engines.

STRATEGY 7: SIC YOUR BOSS ON CO-WORKERS

Talk to your boss about how poorly things are going on a project in which you are not involved in any way. Make stuff up, then cover yourself by saying it's "only what you heard." Get your boss all lathered up, aim him in the right direction, and get out of the way. It might take days for him to find out that everything you said is a lie. But that won't stop him from finding problems with that project once he starts rooting around over there. When he reports back that the problems you mentioned weren't true, say it was all a misunderstanding, then repeat with a rumor about a different project.

STRATEGY 8: MEETING TRAPS

Any time you are in a meeting with anyone, for any topic whatsoever, suggest to the attendees that they should set up some time to talk to your boss about subjects that do not involve you. Find out what the meeting attendees need and then inform them that your boss is a renowned expert in that area, although it might not be obvious from his job title. In all likelihood your boss will agree to meet with these people out of confusion and timidity. With luck, he'll end up on their working committee, thus being too busy to interfere with your daily enjoyment.

STRATEGY 9: BE LOW-MAINTENANCE

One unintended benefit from all the downsizing of the nineties is that there are fewer managers per employee. To make the best of this situation, try to find a job in a department that has several high-maintenance, troublesome employees. You know the type— for some reason the world is always crumbling around them. They are surrounded by crises that need immediate resolution. They park in your boss's doorway every hour and try to remove the oxygen. If you have some of those people in your department, your strategy should be to become the most easily managed, low-maintenance employee your boss has. Create that illusion by going to your boss with easy to-solve problems, along with your recommendations. Example:

> **You:**   Our competitors launched a new product. I recommend that we wait and see what happens.
>
> **Boss:**   Good. Do that.
>
> **You:**   I'm all over it.

Then don't talk to your boss again for a month, creating the impression that everything is under control. You will gain a reputation as the one employee who needs no management assistance, allowing you to perform your unsupervised shirking at any pace you see fit.

STRATEGY 10: BOSS DELETION

For some voice-mail systems, you push the 3 key on your phone to delete a message. The same thing works for deleting live phone conversations with your boss. Next time your boss calls, press the 3 key. Your boss will hear an annoying beep and ask you what it was. Say you didn't hear anything, then do it again. Continue pressing the 3 key until your boss is too upset to continue the conversation.

STRATEGY 11: OPINION SUPPRESSION THERAPY

You can teach your boss to suppress his opinions by making sure he embarrasses himself anytime he opens his mouth. During meetings, ask his opinion about the feasibility of things that have already been done.

Example:

> **You:** Do you think NASA will ever land an unmanned vehicle on Mars?
>
> **Boss:** No way. It's too far.
>
> **You:** You'd better tell NASA. They think they already did it.

STRATEGY 12: BAD ADVICE

If your boss can't tell the difference between good advice and bad advice, give him only bad advice. This will virtually guarantee that he spends less time with you and more time apologizing to people, fixing things he broke, and figuring out why he doesn't get invited to meetings anymore.

STRATEGY 13: SUBMIT YOURSELF FOR AWARDS

Your company probably has some sort of award program for employees who do outstanding work. Take every opportunity to submit yourself for the award, regardless of how shoddy your actual performance is. Eventually your boss will get pressure from someone higher up the command structure to dole out a few employee awards to improve morale. Your boss has to give the

meone, and your co-workers probably aren't any

tanding" than you are. But you will be the path of least

e if you plan it right.

enever you spend money on anything, claim you saved a huge

ant compared to what you originally estimated it would cost. If you buy a new PC for $1,500, submit yourself for an award for not spending $2,000. If that's not a big enough savings, propose a departmentwide policy that all PC purchases be $1,500. Then claim the savings on every machine that might be purchased in the future.

All your boss needs is a flimsy rationalization in order to take the award to his boss for approval. He won't probe your logic too hard because you're solving his problem too.

Once you have the award, you automatically become the front runner for the next round of raises and promotions. In a few months your boss might not recall what the reward was for, but he will remember that you're a bit more "outstanding" than your co-workers.

STRATEGY 14: TURN YOUR BOSS INTO YOUR MINDLESS ZOMBIE SLAVE

Have you noticed that when you yawn, other people yawn too? Or sometimes you'll be in a meeting, and you'll lean on the table with your hands together by your chin, then you notice that other people will do the same thing subconsciously? That's a subtle form of hypnosis. You can develop that skill to a higher degree with a little practice. What I'm about to describe will sound implausible, but I used this method often during my cubicle career (after taking a course in hypnosis), and it works more often than you'd imagine.

You don't have to put someone in a trance to influence behavior. All you need is a basic hypnosis technique called "pacing and leading." Pacing is when you mimic your boss. If he speaks softly, you speak softly. If he uses visual language—like "I see what you mean"—then you use visual language, like "I saw it coming." If your boss leans on his arm, you lean on your arm. You can even learn to match breathing patterns. The more behaviors you pace, the better it works.

Avoid pacing the big, noticeable things, like the way he dresses or the specific malaprops he uses. That will make you look more like a pathetic suck-up than the puppetmaster you are. Stick to the little, subconscious behaviors. And do it every chance you get.

After you've paced your boss for a while—ten minutes is plenty—you're ready to "lead." Test your control by putting your hands in a certain position and seeing if he follows. If he does, his brain is already under your subtle control. At this point, the things you say will seem more persuasive.

If you say something and then your boss says, "I was just thinking that," you can assume you have total control. You won't be able to order him to assassinate anyone, but he might think your ideas are excellent even if they aren't.

Bonus tip: When your boss is standing in front of a group of people, it's fun to pace him until you have control, then act as though your entire body is suddenly very itchy.

STRATEGY 15: PLANT FALSE MEMORIES

This strategy works best with accomplices. Any time your boss asks you why you're doing something a certain way, tell him you discussed it with him last week and he decided this was the way to go. Look surprised and bewildered that he is rehashing this old decision.

If everyone in the office uses the same trick, your boss will believe he is losing his memory. He won't be willing to see a mental-health professional for fear of finding out the worst. If your boss insists that the problem is on your end, don't argue. Just shake your head and mutter, "Same thing Grandpa used to say."

STRATEGY 16: BAD-NEWS INOCULATIONS

If you have mildly bad news for your boss, inoculate him first. You do that by inventing an unverifiable story that is much worse than the real bad news. For example, if the mildly bad news is that your product development is going to be a week late, you might say, "My sources tell me Microsoft is planning to make the same product that we are. It's their top priority."

Wait a few days for the inoculation to take hold, then tell him the mildly bad news about your schedule. Give that a few days to sink in too. Then tell your boss that you did extensive research (on your own time) and found out that the Microsoft rumor was totally false! The good news is that your product will only be a week late.

BOSS-MANAGING STORIES FROM THE FIELD

Here are some stories from people who developed their own methods of boss management.

From: [name withheld]
To: scottadams@aol.com

My boss required semidaily progress reports, and we all know nothing changes that quickly, especially when you work in a group of 300 software engineers on one project.

I created a computer file of status keywords like: 55% complete, process inspection, communication with engineers, advanced investigation, etc. Then I wrote a program that randomly combined the nonsense status phrases based on an algorithm involving the seconds showing on my PC clock. Once created, the program would automatically send the status report to my boss.

Eventually my boss used me as an example of an engineer who was following the process!

From: [name withheld]
To: scottadams@aol.com

I have found a great way to keep my boss convinced I'm working. I have a $10 fake security camera complete with battery-powered blinking red light (stamped "Security Camera") mounted in my cubicle and pointed at me. All my co-workers and my supervisor are convinced I'm working all the time, as who would slouch off if they're being watched!

It also keeps people from stealing pens and using my phone when I'm not there!

From: [name withheld]
To: scottadams@aol.com

Here's what we did to my boss. He bought this new Cadillac (which he was able to afford thanks to our blood, sweat, and tears). Being a sensitive guy, he lorded it over us because we are nothing. Being sensitive employees, every time he would park his beloved baby in his super-important reserved indoor parking spot, we would sneak down there and pour motor oil on the floor beneath his engine. Naturally, he freaked out and we could hear him screaming at the dealership all the way across the office. He took it back to them to fix it. We let it rest two days and resumed the pseudo–oil leak. He took it back again, demanding they fix it or give him a new car. He now wants to sue them. I told him I know of a great mechanic who, for the right price, will guarantee he can fix it.

From: [name withheld]
To: scottadams@aol.com

I once had a boss who was the worst micro-manager in the known universe. He would literally stand behind you and tell you what keys to press on the keyboard. I repro-grammed my keyboard so that nothing he told me to do worked. He finally got the idea and gave up bothering me.

From: [name withheld]
To: scottadams@aol.com

I have a boss who is a hypochondriac. If I don't feel like dealing with him on a given day, the first time I see him, I cough and say, "I think I'm coming down with something." He always leaves me alone for the rest of the day.

From: [name withheld]
To: scottadams@aol.com

I used to have a boss who spent far too much time talking to people when they were trying to get work done. To resolve this problem, my co-workers and I devised a rotating assignment called "Boss Duty." If it was your day, you were obligated to see that the boss was entertained and not communicating to engineers on the critical path of the project. On your "duty day," you were expected to respond within five minutes to e-mail reports of co-workers who were trapped in their offices with the boss. I believe that he never caught on to this productivity enhancement system we installed on his behalf.

From: [name withheld]
To: scottadams@aol.com

One slow day at work in a small store, I was talking to my friend the cashier, and my boss comes up and says, "Why aren't you working?"

I said, "There's nothing to do."

He says, "Pretend you're working."

I said, "YOU pretend I'm working. Then pretend you're taking over for me and I can go home."

From: [name withheld]
To: scottadams@aol.com

I had a boss who wouldn't consider any suggestions made by subordinates. So whenever we had an idea, we told him that it was his boss's idea.

From: [name withheld]
To: scottadams@aol.com

My boss and I were asked to audit a branch office. She wrote the first draft of the audit, which was pretty scathing, and we passed it on to her boss, the VP.

The VP sent it back and asked us to "edit it for tone." So we took the report that was printed single-sided, recopied it double-sided, bound it, and submitted it again. The VP expressed his complete satisfaction with the new, thinner version.

From: [name withheld]
To: scottadams@aol.com

The best method I have found for managing bosses is the tried-and-true Jedi Mind Trick. For example, if your boss asks you, "Have you finished that project yet?" just look your boss straight in the eyes, and with a wave of your hand reply, "These are not the droids that we are looking for, move along."

This proved successful on many occasions during my first job at an investment bank. I became so skilled that I actually trained my fellow employees in the ways of the Force.

From: [name withheld]
To: scottadams@aol.com

When I was a secretary I discovered that the best way to manage my boss (an investment banker) was to borrow the techniques I used as a baby-sitter when I was a teenager. As long as you're firm, unafraid of putting them in their place, and treat them like small children who don't know what's best for them, you can pretty much ensure that things will run the way you want them to.

It also helps if you're the only one who knows their social security number, credit-card numbers, cell phone password, computer password, mother's maiden name, girlfriend's birthday, etc., so that they're forced to depend on you for every aspect of their everyday life. And, of course, when your boss is away on business trips you should rearrange all the files so that you're the only one who knows where anything is.

After a while my boss developed such trust and dependence that he actually called me from an airport to ask if it was the right one, because the plane wasn't there and he hadn't bothered to check his itinerary or even tell the driver which airport to take him to. He'd just gotten into the car like a trusting little lamb and never bothered to look out the window to see where they were going. Naturally he'd taken someone else's car by mistake and had gone to Newark instead of La Guardia. Whoops.

He seemed taken aback when I explained that the best I could do to remedy the situation was to book him on a new flight (under a different name, of course, so that the computer wouldn't nix him) and that actually holding or rerouting the plane was beyond even MY powers!

Don't worry that your boss will not be able to accomplish his duties if he is managed by you. In a good economy, where employees switch companies at the drop of a hat, managers have only one important function:

▶ AVOIDING BEING MEASURED

The biggest threat to workplace happiness is something called the Employee Evaluation. Few things in life are more aggravating than being critically evaluated by the Village Idiot, i.e., your boss. Every time your boss measures you against your objective, it drains a little bit of happiness out of your body.

You could try to find a job where your performance is not measured at all, but those are rare. Your best bet is to get a job where you are measured for all the wrong things, thus allowing you to subvert the system for your personal enjoyment.

For example, in my first job out of college, I was a bank teller. My only measurable objectives involved avoiding screw-ups. Being a well-intentioned rookie, I also tried to provide quick and courteous service, even though it wasn't a measured objective. I handled twice as many customers per shift as other tellers. I also had twice the mistakes and was robbed at gunpoint twice as often (two times in six months). It seemed like I was constantly in trouble. My co-workers, some of whom were later charged with embezzlement, appeared to be model employees. They enjoyed stress-free days and generous raises. Clearly, my strategy of "quick and courteous service" was a loser.

The veteran tellers were clever. They realized that the best way to avoid mistakes—and bank robbers—was to serve the fewest customers possible. The smart tellers developed crafty and elaborate strategies for minimizing customer contact while appearing to be working. During the few minutes per day when they actually helped customers, they would keep the nice ones at the window as long as possible. It was common for my co-workers, many of them single, to flirt shamelessly and try to get dates with any customer who deposited a large check. Meanwhile, I would be trying to explain to angry foreigners why it was in their best interest that the bank didn't let them withdraw their own money.

It took me a long time to realize that I wasn't being more efficient than my co-workers, I was being more stupid. The thing that finally tipped me off to their treachery was the realization that I always ended up waiting on one notoriously difficult customer, against all odds, no matter how many windows were open. When that customer was next in line, my window always opened up first. The customer-from-hell ran a small cash-based business nearby. She was a stern older woman from a country that outlawed smiling centuries ago. She would dump a huge bag of rumpled and filthy money from the day's commerce and scowl at me

while I counted it. Invariably, my count would disagree
The next hour would entail a spirited search for truth
her theories that some of the money might have fallen
cracks while it was being counted. When I confronted my co-
workers about the odds of that customer always ending up at my
window, they confessed that they watched for her in line every
day, then stalled their customers until my window opened. My co-
workers were weasels, but they were smart weasels. And they
knew how to protect their happiness at work.

From: [name withheld]
To: scottadams@aol.com

I work in a technical support group. Our manager decided
that the best measure of our performance is the number of
calls we take in a day. Since we have three phone lines,
our staff has found that using one line to call yourself on
another line will give you credit for a call. It's beautiful.
The tech support center's stats have been rising steadily,
while the number of incoming outside calls has been on an
annual downswing.

It might be inspirational to know that this conflict between the measurer and measured has been raging for thousands of years, and the employees always win. In fact, that's why some of the wonders of the ancient world were so oddly shaped.

For example, scholars have long debated why the pyramids are pointy. One theory is that the pharaoh's marketing department designed the pyramids in the shape of their own heads. Another theory is that the marketing department came up with the name "pyramids," and everyone agreed that it sounded like something pointy. So the engineers wisely built the pyramids with pointy tops; that way they wouldn't have to spend their lives explaining why the buildings weren't called squaramids. They avoided a billion conversations that would have gone like this one:

Tourist: I thought you said you were taking me to the pyramids.

Guide: These *are* the pyramids. For the millionth time today, they are *supposed* to be rectangle-shaped. The pharaoh's marketing department printed the brochures and then it was too late . . . oh, just forget it.

Tourist: I want my money back!

Guide: I hate my job. Just get back on the camel.

Tourist: I call no hump.*

---

*In the first draft of this book, some people were confused by the hump reference. It is intended as a clever allusion to the floor hump in the backseat of a car, but in this case referring to the camel where the hump is harder to avoid. It is not, as some suggested, a reference to the tourist's romantic preferences.

To me, it's obvious that marketing wasn't responsible for the shape of the pyramids. In those days, if your only skill was marketing, your contribution to major construction projects was in the capacity of tile grout. It took thousands of years before people who had no useful skills realized they could earn money by wearing nice clothes and designing deceptive brochures.

The real reason that the pyramids are pointy-shaped is that the pharaohs made the mistake of giving their engineers only two measurable objectives: (1) the size of the base and (2) the height. The pharaohs expected the building to be something in the rectangle family, but that was never specified. It didn't take long for the Egyptian engineers to figure out how to play the game. Every day the pharaoh would get a report from the lead engineer that the pyramid was another ten feet higher and ahead of schedule. It was bonus figs all around.

The engineers weren't afraid of getting in trouble. Back then, the average person had about the same life expectancy as a fruit fly in a blender. There was a good chance the engineers would be dead before the pharaoh found out that the upstairs bonus room was three inches square. In the unlikely event that the pharaoh performed a surprise site visit, it was a simple matter to drop a huge rock on his frail body and flatten him. This happened a lot, apparently, because all the drawings of early Egyptian royalty looked like flattened people.

Although life expectancies have improved a great deal since ancient times, the science of management is limping along pretty much the same, except for one important change:

Jobs are harder to measure now.

In the modern economy, millions of people have the kind of jobs where their contributions are impossible to quantify. They're doing squishy stuff like designing, thinking, planning, positioning, networking, communicating, and creating. Your manager can't see any of those things, much less measure them. But measure he must, because that is what distinguishes managers from inorganic matter.

The danger here is that everything your boss knows about you is based on what he can see.

WHAT YOUR BOSS KNOWS ABOUT YOU

► What you look like

► The number of hours you are in the office

Your outward appearance and your physical location are more important than ever, because that's the only part of your job performance that your boss can see. Your inner talents and the intangible contributions won't have much impact on your career.

You have to satisfy both of your boss's visual requirements—

working long hours and looking good. If you come up short on either of those areas, your boss will be all over you, and you will not be happy. Here's a good example.

From: [name withheld]
To: scottadams@aol.com

This incident happened to a former colleague at a bank. Let's call him "Bob." Bob was assigned an urgent project with very high priority, which involved designing a new product in a very short period. Bob worked 18-hour days for weeks. He treated weekends just like weekdays. He only went home to sleep. The project was completed on time, and Bob's boss, who we'll call "Satan," was congratulated heartily by the bank's executives.

The next week was time for Bob's performance review.

The meeting took five minutes. Satan sat Bob down and said, "Bob, I think you may be a little disappointed with the rating I have given you. Generally speaking, you have been working well; however, there are two problems you have which need to be addressed. First, I have never seen you go a whole day without unbuttoning your shirt and loosening your tie. Second—and this is more important— you have a habit of stretching out at your desk and kicking your shoes off. Frankly, that is offensive. If it weren't for these problems, you would rate a solid 'competent.' As is, you are scruffy, and I'm afraid that means you are 'developing.'"

Bob is now talking with employment agencies.

I can't give you any tips on looking good. I spent most of my career working with engineers. The best clothing suggestion I ever got was from an engineer who always wore ankle-high dress shoes that looked like little boots. His reasoning was that the booties covered his socks completely, so no one knew he always wore the same type of white socks. And since white socks are all interchangeable, he not only looked good, he saved time sorting his laundry. That's all I know about looking good.

But I'm highly qualified to teach you the secret of spending long hours in the office doing almost nothing but pursuing your own happiness. Follow the advice in the coming pages and you can transform your time in the office into a virtual vacation playland.

3

Reverse Telecommuting

I didn't invent the term Reverse Telecommuting, but I wish I had. It refers to the process of bringing your personal work into the office. It's the perfect place for paying bills, playing games, checking on your stock investments, handling errands, calling friends, and making copies. To the casual observer, those things look just like work. Most of it is made possible by your friend, the Internet.

▶ INTERNET CONNECTIONS

If you don't have an Internet connection in your cubicle yet, you must get one. This is the mother lode of all entertainment. If you don't have a job that has a legitimate excuse for an Internet connection, change jobs immediately. Take a cut in pay if you have to. If you're not spending your day playing on the Internet, you're not getting full value from the stockholders.

Many companies monitor how employees use the Internet. Managers can get reports of who has been looking at what. Some companies go further, blocking access to entertainment-oriented Websites. Avoid that sort of company at all costs.

When you interview for your new job, ask if they have unmonitored Internet connections for employees. If the interviewer says yes, pump your arm in the air and yell "Woo-hoo!!" It's good to show enthusiasm during interviews. Then ask if the company offers in-office chair massages. If the interviewer says yes, insist on getting yours now, then strip to the waist. That is the sort of company you want to work for. Don't settle for less.

▶ CUBICLE SEX RUMORS

You don't need gadgets to have fun in your cubicle. I've heard many rumors of employees who had sex in their cubicles during work hours. If you play your cards right, you might be lucky enough to hear some rumors too. You don't have any hope of having actual sex in your cubicle. I've come to believe that no one ever has. But you might hear some good rumors, and that's entertainment too.

Rumors of sex in cubicles are like rumors of people who joined the Mile High Club—the people who claim to have had sex on airplanes in flight. I have flown many times and never seen anyone having sex. If all the people who claim to have gotten lucky during commercial flights are telling the truth, I need to get a new travel agent. All I get on my flights are tiny pretzels. I'm lucky if I can get my carry-on luggage in the overhead bin, much less have vigorous unprotected sex with another passenger. I have real trouble believing anyone else is doing the wild thing up there.

I suppose it's possible that the pilots are having sex up in the cockpit. That would explain all the turbulence on clear days, and the fact that they always sound like Charlie Brown's teachers on the announcements.

> Out of your left-side window you can see . . . MWA MWA MWA . . . Grand Tetons . . . MWA MWA MWA . . . French Lick.

► CUBICLE YOGA

Tell your boss that yoga is part of the company's recommended ergonomic safety program. If you don't know how to do yoga, don't worry. I'll teach you the basics here. Believe it or not, I know more about yoga than I know about economics. There are two types of yoga:

TWO TYPES OF YOGA

1. The kind that hurts like crazy

2. The kind that looks like you're sleeping

I recommend the second type. The tough part about yoga is keeping your head balanced after you fall asleep. The yoga masters have learned to sleep for days without allowing their heads to fall over and snap their tiny necks. Until you develop that level of control, consider wearing a neck brace—the kind used by accident victims. That will keep your head upright so you can sleep comfortably in your chair. Tell everyone you got injured skiing. They'll think you're a sporty risk taker. You'll get some sympathy as well as respect. If you don't feel comfortable with that sort of lie, just wear a turtleneck to cover the neck brace.

If you're worried that your yoga isn't moving you closer to enlightenment, try adding a mantra. A mantra is a word you repeat over and over again until you fall asleep. I recommend the mantra I used every day of work for seventeen years: home . . . home . . . home. . . .

Once you've mastered the art of sleeping while sitting up, combine that skill with the technique described below and you will be on your way to career success.

From: [name withheld]
To: scottadams@aol.com

Four years ago I was hired as a consultant. I was told there was an incredible number of projects waiting to be done. I sat there for three weeks before I figured out that there was no work to do.

I used the Windows recorder on my PC to record moving Windows, picking up applications and closing them. I sat there for hours with my hand on the mouse, just staring at the moving screen. Eventually they hired me as a project manager because I was the only one working!

▶ MORE SLEEPING TIPS

Tell everyone in the office that you need to wear dark sunglasses all day to protect your eyes. Not only will you seem ultra-cool but you'll never have to miss another minute of sleep during the workday. If you're worried that your nonresponsiveness during meetings will give you away, apparently you've never been to a meeting. There's always at least one person who says nothing. That person could be you. The only real risk is that people will think you're a worthless sponge-person and not so much a valuable team player.

To counter that accurate perception, I recommend using the "knowing grin" during your rare waking moments. The knowing grin is a method I developed to make myself seem smarter than I really am. The way it works is you wait until someone says something incomprehensible during a meeting and then you smile slightly, as though you know exactly what it means. Make sure everyone else sees you do it. To the ignorant observers it will seem that you understand something that confuses everyone else at the meeting. Moreover, you understand it at such a deep level that you can see the humor and irony behind it too. You are a complex person who operates on many levels. Not a worthless sponge-person.

The grin sends a signal that you are the quiet, confident type who does not need to prove anything by talking. That is all the misdirection you need in order to sleep through long stretches of any meeting without attracting attention.

If you're asked a question, you can always count on one of your co-workers to cut you off and dazzle the room with an assortment of factual inaccuracies and misunderstandings. It's no different from being awake.

If you don't look good in dark glasses, here are some other techniques that can help you get the rest you deserve without bowing to your employer's irrational insistence on productivity.

From: [name withheld]
To: scottadams@aol.com

The best way to get a nap in at the office was practiced by one of my friends. We have actual offices with doors that shut. He would go into his office after lunch and "spill" his paper-clip holder about six feet from the door. Then he would lie down and go to sleep with his feet against the door and his hand in the pile of paper clips. If anyone knocked, he would quickly rise to his hands and knees and shout, "Come in . . . excuse me . . . I'm picking up a little spill here."

From: [name withheld]
To: scottadams@aol.com

A way to sleep on the job I learned about 35 years ago, and it still works! Place a piece of paper on the floor in the foot space by your desk. Let the arm nearest the paper hang down toward the floor while using the other arm as a pillow for your head at the edge of the desk.

Place your head on your arm and go to sleep. As soon as you hear someone walk into your office, make a slight grunting sound as you extend the hanging arm toward the piece of paper and pick it up. It really does seem as though you were just caught in the act of picking up a piece of paper that had fallen on the floor. I've used it many times, and the fact that I'm unemployed today had nothing to do with its use, honest!

▶ MULTISHIRKING

If you don't have a hands-free headset for your telephone, get one, even if you have to use your own money. Once you're properly equipped, you can make personal phone calls while simultaneously using your computer for personal entertainment. To the passerby, it appears that you are doing two work-related activities at once. But in reality you are doing what one *Dilbert* reader calls multishirking, i.e., doing two nonwork activities at once.

Multishirking is not only fun; it doubles the odds that an observer will think you're doing at least one work-related activity.

▶ PRETENDING TO WORK

There are many times during the workday when you wish you could be paid for doing nothing but wandering around the hallway. You can achieve that dream. All you need are the right tools.

From: [name withheld]
To: scottadams@aol.com

To avoid work, walk around with a flashlight and a clipboard full of papers. Inspect your work area, occasionally stopping, shining the light at the ceiling, then writing gibberish on the clipboard.

Clipboards and flashlights are a good start, but to be more convincing, carry a tape measure and a large funnel. If anyone asks you what you're doing, just shake your head and say, "You don't want to know." You can use this approach successfully by carrying just about any two unrelated items, such as a car battery and a ball of twine, or a paint roller and jar of honey. A person carrying that sort of combination is sending the message, "I have a long and sad story to tell, if only someone had an hour or two to listen."

From: [name withheld]
To: scottadams@aol.com

Here are some of my favorite ways to pretend to work.

▶ Erase and rewrite stuff on your dry erase board.
▶ Reshift the Post-it notes and other crap on your desk a couple of times a day.
▶ If possible, always wait for the boss to go to lunch first, then leave immediately thereafter. That way you can get at least a ninety-minute lunch without the boss knowing exactly how long you've been gone.
▶ Pretend to work by spending roughly twenty minutes typing smart-ass comments to nationally known cartoonists while in full view of everyone.

From: [name withheld]
To: scottadams@aol.com

I work for the highway department. If I want to look like
I'm working, all I do is stand on the edge of the road as
though I'm waiting for a break in traffic so that I can cross
the street. When there are no cars blocking my way, no
one is there to see that I am actually daydreaming.

► **INVENTIONS NEEDED**

The office is already well equipped for entertainment, but
there are several inventions needed before cubicle dwellers can
achieve complete nirvana at work.

CUBISCOPE

I'd like to see someone invent what I call the Cubiscope. It's a
periscope device for the cubicle, with a simple video camera on
the top of a telescoping pole. The user controls the raising, lower-
ing, and direction of the camera from a software control panel on
the PC. The camera would send a picture to a small window on
your screen. This would be invaluable for notifying you of any
approaching bosses or annoying co-workers. You could have
hours of fun while searching for targets to torpedo. Ideally, the
software should show crosshairs so you can lock on and destroy
passersby, at least in a virtual sense. Here's how it could work:
The software could compare the video background scene before
and after your target entered the field. Then it could generate an

image of the torpedoes firing, followed by a virtual explosion on-screen. The software would immediately switch the video image back to view the way it looked a moment before the target entered. It would look like you vaporized your victim. The more satisfying annihilations could be saved to video files for later playback.

MOTION DETECTOR

Another much needed invention is a cubicle motion detector with an infrared link to your computer. There are at least three applications that I can imagine with this device. If you're playing video games or surfing the Web on company time, sometimes you don't hear people sneak up behind you. That can be bad for your career. With the motion detector, a signal can be sent to your computer at the speed of light. Speed is important here. When anyone approaches, the motion sensor triggers a background program on your PC that instantly minimizes your game window and brings a work-related screen to the front. It would become literally impossible for anyone to sneak up and catch you playing games.

Another use for the motion detector is to scare people who sneak into your cubicle when you aren't there. You could have a program linked to the motion detector that played a loud sound file when anyone came within your boundaries:

> **You have entered Scott Adams's cubicle. Do not leave things on his chair. Do not make long-distance calls on his phone. Do not borrow his computer manuals. Do not chew on his pen cap while leaving a note. Do not put toxic waste in his recycling container. Get out now.**

Thirdly, your motion detector could be part of a stupidity detector, like Dogbert's invention here.

POOR MAN'S CABLE TV

I would like someone to invent a subscription service for cubicle dwellers that lets them use their telephones to receive audio of their favorite TV and radio programs. The subscriber would call a local number, then select the channel by pressing keys on the phone. You could call up your favorite soap opera or talk show, lean back, close your eyes, and enjoy the show. You wouldn't miss much by having no pictures to look at. Regis and Kathie Lee don't change that much from day to day. And remember, the alternative is usually work.

Another application, using a similar service, would be to have a dial-in channel programmed with random business phrases that go on forever. Dial into that channel, switch on the speakerphone, and pretend to be on a conference call. This gives you the moral authority to shoo off anyone who comes within hearing distance.

STEALTH BOOKS

I'd like to see books that are printed on regular paper, the kind that comes out of the copy machine. You could be sitting four feet away from your boss, reading a bodice-ripping romance novel, and still look like the hardest-working employee in the room, especially if you're red and perspiring. Ideally, the "book" would include randomly highlighted phrases, to give it that studied look. It would be packaged with a yellow marker so the reader can appear poised for additional highlighting at any moment. The text could include stage notes that remind the reader to groan or sigh in a work-related way at strategic intervals. For example:

> The pirate swept her off her feet and carried her up the marble stairway to the master bedroom where he **[reader note: exhale sharply and pretend to highlight something]** shook her hand and then left to play point guard in the midnight basketball league.

Another source of leisure reading on company time is public-domain books that are on the Internet, courtesy of Project Gutenberg at *http://promo.net/pg*. Use your Web browser at home to download the text of classic books whose copyrights have expired. Then e-mail the text to yourself at your office, or load it on your laptop. You'll be able to mentally escape the oppression of your office by enjoying the feel-good writing of Dickens.

4

Laughter at the Expense of Others

The quickest way to increase your happiness at work is through the magic of laughter. You already know that laughter improves your mood, but scientists have discovered that it's good for your health too. I think scientists base that conclusion on studies that indicate no one is ever laughing at the time of death.

Scientists don't specify which sources of laughter are better than others, health-wise, so I recommend laughing at other people—your co-workers in particular—at least until we have more data. If you know any scientists, you can laugh at them too. They won't take it personally because they'll understand you're doing it for medical reasons.

From a purely quantitative standpoint, it makes more sense to laugh at other people than to laugh at yourself. You're only one person, whereas there are new batches of "other people" born every minute, many of whom are hilarious without even trying.

If your co-workers aren't providing you with all the entertainment that you desire, don't be satisfied with that situation. You must learn to nurture the humor potential in your co-workers—like a farmer nurtures a cow, except without touching their nipples.

Farming is a good analogy, and one that I know quite well. I worked on my uncle's dairy farm when I was a kid. I became quite an expert in all things cow-related. All of the lessons that apply to cows can be applied to coworkers. There are many parallels. For example, the definition of a cow is "a big dumb mammal that eats grain and turns it into manure." The definition of a co-worker is "a big dumb mammal that eats doughnuts and turns them into Powerpoint slides." Now, you could argue that a doughnut is different from grain—because sugar and heat are added to make a doughnut—but I think that's splitting hairs.

One of my primary duties on the farm was to round up the cows from the godforsaken swamp that my uncle called the pasture. During the day, the cows would hang out in the pasture, chewing their cud. (Cud is the cow word for gum.) In the early evening, the cows had to be rounded up and taken to the barn for milking. It was my job to get them to the barn. I didn't work alone; I had a cow-worker: a highly trained farm dog named Ringo. The cows respected Ringo. He was a natural leader. When he barked, the cows would instantly line up at the barn door and offer to milk themselves. The cows had far less respect for me. I got an entirely different level of cooperation on the days I worked alone, when, for example, Ringo was driving the truck into town to get supplies.

My solo attempts at cow herding seemed to drive the cows deeper into hiding. They became masters of disguise. Some would submerge themselves in swamp water and breath through tubes. Others ran away to become guests on talk shows, where they got makeovers, then blended into society.

My preferred method of cow herding involved yelling an unintelligible phrase that had been handed down, farmer to farmer, for decades. It goes something like this: KEWBOSSIE!! KEWBOSSIE!! No one really knows what that means, especially the cows, who were busy building underground tunnel cities. My other method was to chase each cow with a menacing stick. Everyone who worked on the farm got to make his or her own menacing stick, using trees grown especially for that purpose. You wanted just the right mix of stiffness, length, and aerodynamic properties. (What might seem to city slickers as a system of planned cruelty to animals was something we called "farming.") One by one, I would seek out each hiding cow and whack it vigorously with my menacing stick, while yelling KEWBOSSIE!! KEWBOSSIE!!

As you might expect, this had no impact whatsoever. So I ended up waiting until Ringo was done buying supplies, cooking dinner, and upgrading the electrical systems in the barn. He'd wander over, bark twice, and look at me like he thought I was a huge pile of Powerpoint slides. It was humiliating, really. And it was perfect preparation for my life in corporate America. Those cows taught me valuable lessons about the joy of yanking other people's chains.

▶ YANKING THE CHAINS OF YOUR CO-WORKERS

One excellent way to entertain yourself at work is to constantly bring up topics that you know will set your co-workers into spastic fits. For example, if you work with someone who is a passionate environmentalist, start your next meeting by pointing out how your project might wipe out a particular species of salamander. Dismiss the problem by saying it doesn't matter because all bugs look the same. Then sit back and watch the fun.

Chain-yanking works best when you take advantage of the stereotypical tendencies of people from different disciplines. For example, people in marketing are trained to put form over substance, so customers don't realize how much they're getting reamed. People who work in technical fields are almost the opposite. They're trained to eliminate the frivolous. That's why it's fun to put marketing people and technical people in the same room and get them torqued up. Here are some fun things to say to those and other professionals:

FUN THINGS TO SAY TO MARKETING PEOPLE

▶ "Why don't we just tell the customers the truth?"

▶ "I noticed that some words are spelled wrong on the new brochures. Is it okay if we correct them with a pen and send them out?"

▶ "I can see your fillings when you talk!"

FUN THINGS TO SAY TO TECHNICAL PEOPLE

▶ "We're only making a few changes. There's no reason to test it again."

▶ "Does everyone agree that Microsoft makes the best software?"

▶ "You don't need *another* technical training class. You went to one last year."

▶ "I need to take your only prototype with me to show to a customer. I won't lose it."

▶ "I don't know what I need, but if you put something

together based on this conversation, I'll let you know if you got it right."

FUN THINGS TO SAY TO ACCOUNTING PEOPLE

- ▶ "If my actual expenses don't match the budget, isn't that proof that the budget process is a sham?"

- ▶ "Give me the money now and I'll get the budget approvals later."

- ▶ "What do you mean you can't give me more money in my budget? Just change the numbers on the spreadsheet."

- ▶ "I had a budget surplus at the end of the year, but don't worry—I took care of it."

- ▶ "Is it okay if I spend my depreciation budget on travel?"

FUN THINGS TO SAY TO SALESPEOPLE

- ▶ "Your advance sales are excellent, but we changed our mind about making that product."

- ▶ "We should redesign your compensation plan to give you more incentives."

- ▶ "Why don't you take one of the engineers to meet with your customers?"

▶ STARTING FALSE RUMORS FOR FUN

It's fun to spread false rumors that cause senseless panic in the office. This is a form of employee motivation that isn't discussed much in the popular literature. If you follow my excellent advice, you can make your co-workers run around and cluck like a bunch of chickens who just drank a keg of coffee and rolled around in itching powder. This is every bit as entertaining as it sounds.

It's best to leave some vagueness in your rumors so your gullible co-workers can fill in the holes with whatever scares them the most. That's a trick I learned when I was a Navy SEAL. Actually, technically, I learned the trick as a budget analyst at a big bank. But that is similar to being a Navy SEAL.*

Budget analysts were usually the first to know of any big changes in company plans. We were sworn to secrecy, but that didn't limit our ability to leave frightening clues of impending doom.

How to Frighten Co-Workers:

Me: Bob, I'll need your budget projections by tomorrow. It's urgent.

Bob: Okay.

Me: Ted, same thing. I *must* have your projections by tomorrow.

Ted: Will do.

Milton: I guess you need my budget projections tomorrow too, huh?

Me: Whatever.

---

*Navy SEALs have a rule about never leaving a fallen buddy behind. Budget analysts typically torture their own wounded just to watch them yell. Otherwise, it's similar.

Speaking of South Dakota, the best rumors are the ones that—if true—would make your job approximately as enjoyable as tongue-washing the faces of the presidents on Mount Rushmore, in February, while your supervisor yells, "Don't forget the nostrils!"

Here are some rumors that will get your co-workers' clucking:

RELOCATION RUMORS

Tell your co-workers that you heard the company is relocating to a place where the cost of living is VERY reasonable. You don't know the specifics, but you did hear that a five-bedroom home with an animal-carcass roof can be purchased for under four dollars. You've heard that crime in this new place is virtually nonexistent, largely because criminals prefer to reside in inner cities where they will be slain in drive-by shootings. The worse thing that can happen in the new location is that you get abducted in your sleep and forced to marry a reindeer farmer. That might seem unpleasant if you don't like beard stubble, but you get all the free deer cheese you want.

And don't worry that the weather report is routinely expressed in terms of suicide rates. Employees will be given the option of moving to this place or accepting a generous retirement package. The generous package consists of your personal belongings shoved in a Hefty bag and heaved from the roof onto the heads of litigious pedestrians.

The company realizes that relocation can be stressful. They plan to address the stress problem head-on by holding a mandatory weekend conference called "Don't Be Afraid of Change." Be prepared to do a skit entitled "The Aerobic Benefits of Fear."

NEW BOSS RUMOR

Start a rumor that you're getting a new boss who is twenty-three years old. Tell everyone that she was a nail-care specialist until she was "discovered" by your philandering CEO. Her management experience includes raising dozens of dogs in her apartment until the Humane Society took them away.

She has been quoted as saying, "I've managed cuticles for over seven months. How different could cubicles be? That's just one letter difference."

She has a record of working well with executives, including your married CEO, the principal of her high school, and a guy who always dressed in brown—who she thinks was an important executive because he got permission to use a UPS truck for their dates.

She doesn't have much formal education, but you could say she did attend the school of hard knocks—mostly in the back of the UPS truck.

HANDWRITING ANALYSIS RUMOR

Tell co-workers that you are collecting handwriting samples for the security department but you aren't allowed to say why. If a co-worker insists on knowing why, take him aside and explain that the company has a handwriting expert who can detect deviant sexual preferences by looking at writing samples. According to the expert, deviants have sloppy handwriting and tend to spell words incorrectly. Ask the person to write this sentence as you dictate it: "The picnickers ate broccoli on a toboggan." If your victim asks how to spell any of those words, gasp audibly and scurry away with a frightened look.

BOSS GENDER-CHANGE RUMOR

Tell new employees that your boss had a sex-change operation and is hypersensitive about any use of gender-specific pronouns like "he" or "she." Inform the new employees to use only gender-neutral words like "it" and "they" to avoid making a scene.

TAPED CONVERSATIONS RUMOR

Tell gullible co-workers that sometimes management will wire an employee with hidden microphones to gather incriminating information about other employees. You can tell which employees are wearing a wire because they are the ones who ask a lot of questions. Sometimes they'll act confused just to make you repeat yourself.

▶ PROBLEMS ARE ENTERTAINMENT IN DISGUISE

Perhaps your boss has told you that problems are really opportunities in disguise. It's true, but only if the problems belong to other people. Those problems are indeed opportunities for you to get free entertainment. I think you'll agree there is no laugh that is quite as satisfying as the one you get at the expense of your co-workers.

For example, if a co-worker came to you in distress and said,

"It's an emergency! I need your help to do something that I would have done last week, if only my brain weren't made of pork rinds!" (Your co-worker might word it differently, probably saying "wasn't" instead of "weren't.")

Your response—also known as your "opportunity"—might sound something like, "**HA** HA HA HA HA HA!!!" Or, if you're dyslexic like me, it might sound something like, "HA **HA** HA HA HA HA!!!"

Make sure your co-workers don't detect any traces of empathy as you listen to their problems. Everyone knows that if you have empathy, you probably have the capacity for guilt too. And guilt is all your co-workers need in order to turn you into their personal problem-solving slave. They'll control you by creating an endless series of self-inflicted disasters that only you can fix. I call it the "Jumping off a Ledge" strategy. The metaphor is this: You're walking along the sidewalk when a co-worker jumps off a third-story ledge above you. He screams your name as he plummets. Somehow (because this is a poorly constructed metaphor) you know this isn't a suicide attempt; it's just your idiot co-worker's way of taking a shortcut to his car.

Should you do nothing and watch him fall, thus proving to everyone that you are not a team player? Or do you cushion his fall with your body, thus proving to everyone that jumping on your head is an acceptable shortcut?

Fortunately, those aren't your only options. I recommend a more humorous approach: Act as though you are ***trying*** to catch the falling body but you're too spastic to get to the right spot on time. This solution has many advantages: You won't get hurt. You won't appear selfish. No one will be quick to try that shortcut again. You'll have a funny story to tell, especially when you act out your spastic part. And best yet—you'll be the first one to get any spare change that's freed up by the impact.

▶ INFECTING YOUR CO-WORKERS

Just because you're sick, that's no reason to stay home. The body is an amazing machine, capable of enduring the most ghastly germs and bacteria until they can be safely transferred to your co-workers. If you can move at all, you might as well go to work and enjoy one of the few legal ways you can intentionally cause bodily harm to other people.

Disease can be spread in many ways, including insect bites, unwashed hands, mad cows, ISO 9000, unsafe sex, Israeli assassination teams, and shared whistles. Most of those methods I can't recommend. For example, I don't know anyone who would want to spread disease by biting insects. Your best bet is a combination of unwashed hands and projectile coughing.

The cough has one big advantage over the sneeze. People don't say "God bless you" when you cough. That's important because you really don't want to attract God's attention in this situation. I realize he's omnipotent and omniscient and all that, so technically he could watch *everything* if he wanted to. But if I were a supreme being I would spend very little time looking at sick people. I'd have hobbies, such as hunting.

Having an illness at work is like having a super power but without the burden of being raised by kindly farmers who ruin your fun by giving you a bunch of ethics. When you're germ-laden, you're like the evil criminals who escaped jail on Krypton just before the planet exploded. People fear you when you're sick. Try wearing a cape and tall boots to accentuate the effect. Then yell "Bow before me!" before you cough on a co-worker.

▶ WASTEBASKET FUN

If you work in a cubicle, you probably have only one tiny trash receptacle. Or if your company cares about the environment, it's called a recycling container. In either case, it gets hauled to the landfill in huge trucks and emptied onto the heads of seagulls.

The problem is that you have several tons of unwieldy trash coming into your cubicle each day. You've got old binders, junk mail, cardboard, vendor giveaways, newspapers, lunch scraps, you name it. Your garbage far exceeds your receptacle's capacity. To further complicate things, your company probably has rules about what kind of trash is "acceptable" for your trash receptacle. This is where the challenge comes in.

Let's say, just for the sake of example, that you have a six-gallon jug of anthrax virus that you don't need anymore. What do you do with it? There's probably some corporate guideline about this sort of thing, but it would take all day to track down someone with an answer. And you know the answer would be one you don't want to hear:

Anthrax Policy

All anthrax virus must be wrapped in a radioactive asbestos blanket and buried in a limestone quarry for ten thousand years. Have all forms notarized. Keep a tickler file.

You will weigh the limestone-quarry option carefully and compare it to the alternative: putting the anthrax jug in someone else's cubicle before you go home at night. That person will probably do the same thing to someone else the next day. Eventually the jug will find someone who is uncaring enough to dump it in the water fountain on another floor. That's the best you can hope for; the anthrax is gone and your conscience is clear.

The process is the same for nonliquid refuse, such as banana peels and dead animals. As long as there are lazy people who go home sooner than you do, there is no limit to your opportunities for creative trash disposal.

Some companies supply attractive recycling bins for each cubicle. At Pacific Bell, one of my co-workers decided that the recycling bin was an excellent place to keep his most important documents during the day. This method worked very well until one night when he forgot to take the important documents out of the recycling bin and put them in his drawer before he left for the night. Somewhere in Michigan a little girl is blowing her nose with his important documents. This is the sort of mistake that my co-worker found difficult to blame on someone else, but that did not stop him from trying. He called the building maintenance manager and chewed him out for stupidly recycling the documents that were in the recycling bin.

This story suggests a good prank to play on new hires. Tell them the bins labeled "recycling" are intended for the important documents that you use over and over again (hence the name "recycling"). Get accomplices to put their important documents in their recycling bins during the day too, so the pattern is well established for the rookie. If the new employee gets suspicious of what "recycling" really means, tell him it's a word that comes from Quality training. Offer to sign him up for a class if he wants to get more details. The new employee will quickly fall in line for fear of being trained. When your victim finds out his important documents have disappeared, suggest that he take it up with the building maintenance manager.

▶ COMPLAINING TO THE OMBUDSMAN

For those of you who do not work at large companies, let me explain what an ombudsman is. As the name implies, an ombudsman is what you get when you combine words from the diverse fields of meditation, beer, and something called "sman." An ombudsman's job is to listen to the complaints of employees on any ethical matter, then recommend solutions that help the employee move from a feeling of discomfort to a feeling of utter despair.

Example:

Employee: My boss is a sadistic, demented, Satan worshiper. He's using his position of power to create an army of devil-slaves.

Ombudsman: Have you tried talking to your boss about your feelings?

Employee: Yes, once, but he threw goat blood on me, drugged me, then tied me to his credenza for some sort of ceremony that I don't fully remember.

Ombudsman: I'll send him a letter to tell him our policy about that sort of thing.

Employee: But then he'll know I complained and he'll kill me.

Ombudsman: Well, if you prefer, I'll just do nothing.

Employee: That's what you said last time I came here. Do you ever do anything?

Ombudsman: I tried that once. It didn't work out.

That's what the normal ombudsman experience is like. But you can have fun with your ombudsman by inventing imaginary ethical dilemmas. Here are some good questions for your ombudsman.

QUESTIONS FOR THE OMBUDSMAN

▶ Every one of my co-workers is mentally undressing me. It makes me feel like a . . . what the . . . what are YOU looking at??!!

▶ One of our vendors gave me a sports utility vehicle. But it's not the color I wanted. Is it okay if I kidnap his dog?

▶ When I phone in a bomb threat to the office, is it wrong to use my company calling card?

▶ I discovered that my boss has been embezzling from the company. Should I stop dating him?

▶ My travel allowance for food is $30 per day. Can I spend some of it on drugs if I eat them?

▶ THE JOY OF BAD IDEAS

Thinking is easier than working. And the best kind of thinking is the kind where you don't have to write anything down, i.e., "meeting thinking." When you think up an idea during a meeting, all you have to do is blurt it out. You won't have to involve any parts of your body except your mouth and maybe your brain stem.

The quality of your ideas is irrelevant. You can get away with spewing bad ideas all day because no one can tell the difference between a great idea and a bad idea. For example, imagine if Picasso had to explain his ideas to some sort of art committee before starting each new painting.

Picasso: I'm thinking of going in a whole new direction.

Committee: That's terrific. It sounds very artistic. Tell us more.

Picasso: I think my portraits should have the eyes on the same side of the head sometimes.

Committee: Uh-huh.

Picasso: And the drawings should look like scribbles. It's hard to explain, but trust me, it will look great!

Committee: Couldn't you draw dinosaurs instead? They're very popular.

Picasso: No, trust me, I have something here.

Committee: Or how about fruit? Now *that's* art. Or dinosaurs eating fruit! Or how about one of the dinosaurs slips on a banana peel and says, "I've fallen and I can't get up."

With that, the committee members high-five one another and vote on the dinosaur painting. Picasso takes out his Swiss Army knife and tries to cut off his ear, stopping only when he is reminded that Van Gogh was the one who did that.

The most entertaining ideas are the kind that make your co-workers do unnecessary work. Try to limit your ideas to ones that sound logical on some level but are clearly failures waiting to happen.

LOGICAL-SOUNDING IDEAS

▶ Include the legal department in your next brainstorming session.

▶ Ask the marketing department if they'll give you some of their budget.

▶ Invade Russia in the winter.

If your ideas have any trace of logic, your co-workers will be unable to defend themselves to your boss. You'll enjoy the immediate satisfaction of watching them squirm, followed by the long-term satisfaction of watching them flail helplessly as they slide toward doom.

▶ PRETENDING TO BE PSYCHIC

When you move to a new job, even if it's within the same company, use the opportunity to reinvent yourself. As far as your new co-workers know, you're not lazy, unscrupulous, and selfish. It could take them days to figure that out. In the meantime, you can pretend to have many admirable attributes and no one will be the wiser. I recommend pretending to be a psychic.

It's easy to be a psychic. Start with easy things. When you meet a new guy, glance at his company ID badge and say, "You look like a Dave. Am I right?" Eighty percent of the people you try this on will realize you're looking at the ID and laugh at your lame joke, thus thinking you are highly intelligent because you use humor. The other 20 percent will offer to shave their heads and give you all of their worldly possessions. Remember, we're talking about a general population where a third of the people are planning their lives around the zodiac. It won't take many demonstrations of supernatural talent before you're running your own cult.

Here's another psychic trick I learned. I can correctly call a coin flip 100 percent of the time, as long as I'm the one flipping the coin. I had to learn this trick because I lose all coin flips unless I cheat. People are dumb enough to let me be the coin flipper only about half of the time, so statistically it all works out.

Here's how to rig a coin flip. Always use a new United States quarter. Don't use any other coin. A new quarter feels distinctly smooth on the George Washington side and distinctly ridgy on the eagle side. See for yourself. Put a new quarter in your palm and run your second-smallest finger from the same hand across its surface. With a little practice you can tell the smooth side from the ridgy side almost every time without looking. Now, all you need is a minor diversion during the coin toss so you have time to check the coin in your hand with your finger before slapping it down.

Flip the coin high in the air, then reach out and snatch it on the way down, about head level. Bring your other arm up so you can slap the coin on your arm. Look the other person in the eye and say, "The coin is . . ." This slight delay gives you enough time to run your finger across the surface of the quarter. Slap the coin on your wrist and keep it covered. The side opposite the one you felt will now be showing when you remove your hand.

(Note: If there are any old girlfriends of mine reading this, I think we can look back now and laugh.)

I've also developed a system for reading minds. It's a way to tell if people are lying about their guilt. The method is about 90 percent accurate. All you do is unexpectedly ask the most direct question you can, then listen for which of two possible approaches the person uses to respond. For example, you might say, "Did you kill your neighbor?"

Innocent people answer that sort of question by saying, "No, I didn't!" or "Are you &%#$ crazy?" or "I can't believe you're even asking me that."

Guilty people say, "Whatever gave you that idea?" or "There's no evidence of that!" or "Why would you even ask such a thing?" or "Did someone say I did?"

The main difference is that the guilty people are attacking the evidence, not denying the event. Innocent people will deny the event and get mad at the person who asked the question. If you get a mixture of responses, give more weight to what the person says first. You will be astounded at how well this method works.

For practice, you can play this game at home when you watch any news-oriented show in which people are being asked about their guilt. When Mike Wallace shoves the microphone in front of some widow-cheating scumbag, just listen to the choice of words the scumbag uses to defend himself:

Mike Wallace: Did you cheat those senior citizens?

Scumbag: There's no reliable evidence of that!

After some practice with the television, when you think you have the hang of it, try an ambush interview on your boss.

You: Is the project I'm working on doomed by upcoming budget cuts?

Boss: Whatever gave you that idea?

Once you've established your powers of mind reading, enhance your psychic credentials by making predictions that are spookily accurate. This is easier than you might think. Here are some predictions that will fit any business situation with 90 percent accuracy:

FOOLPROOF BUSINESS PREDICTIONS

▶ The department will be reorganized within six months, for no compelling reason.

▶ The biggest weasel in the department will be promoted soon.

▶ The project will be delayed by huge unforeseen obstacles.

▶ The computer network will experience many outages.

▶ The new employee who had so much promise will turn out to be ineffective.

▶ The project will cost more than anyone expected.

You can also take advantage of stereotypes to make it appear as though you can read minds. The trick is to avoid the most obvious guesses and go for the ones that are at one remove. For example, let's say you meet a co-worker and notice he is wearing cowboy boots under his suit. The obvious insight would be, "Brent, I'll bet you like country music." But no one will think you're psychic with that sort of obvious guess. Instead, say, "Brent, I've got a hunch that you like dogs."

The dog prediction will be correct because all people who wear cowboy boots also like dogs. Boot-wearing men generally think that cats are girlie pets.

Now let's say you meet a co-worker who has a gigantic butt. You could go for the obvious and say, "I predict that you like to eat ice cream." But that's not very psychic. And it might be construed as an insult, thus thwarting your attempt to build goodwill. A better strategy would be to say, "Randy, I'm just guessing, but I think you really enjoy renting movies and watching them at home."

This will be exactly correct, because all people with large butts enjoy renting videos and watching them at home. By moving your stereotype one step away from the obvious, you avoid insult while retaining all of your accuracy.

▶ BEING A TECHNOLOGY PRIMA DONNA

There's never been a better time in history to be a Technology Prima Donna. Good employees are hard to find, but good employees who understand technology are even rarer. If you have any technical skill at all—or you can fake it—take full advantage of the raw power and happiness that comes with being a Technology Prima Donna.

If I were a famous psychologist—and thus free to make up stuff and still be credible—I would propose two possible explanations for why Technology Prima Donnas get away with their behavior. The most obvious is that everyone believes Technology Prima Donnas are capable of going on a killing spree, so it's a good idea to give them what they want. But there's another theory that is equally plausible: Most people foolishly believe "You get what you pay for."

The Technology Prima Donna makes you "pay" a higher psychological price for knowing him or her. Therefore you rationalize that there must be some value to justify the high price. (I would be an excellent fake psychologist.) If the Technology Prima Donna in your department doesn't get fired right away, you start to think the person must have some substantial hidden talents that make the abuse worthwhile. Within a month, you're telling other people what a genius this sociopath is. The Technology Prima Donna's reputation spreads. Soon it becomes impossible to fire the Technology Prima Donna because everyone will think the business depends on this one person.

Common sense might tell you that people who act like Technology Prima Donnas would be killed by angry mobs while the police turn a blind eye. But it doesn't work that way. Technology Prima Donnas are treated as stars and given extra money and larger cubicles. Sometimes even offices! As a worker, your choice is to suffer the indignities of interacting with Technology Prima Donnas or to become one yourself. I suggest becoming one. All you really lose is friends, and you can get more of those on the Internet.*

Most departments can survive having only one or two

---

*The Internet is the best place to find friends, because you can pretend to be someone else. Your Internet friends will also be pretending to be other people, so in essence you will be creating fake people who will be friends with each other, but that's close enough. At least no one will ask to borrow your stuff.

Technology Prima Donnas, so make sure you're one of them. It won't be hard to fool your boss into thinking you're a Technology Prima Donna if you follow these guidelines:

HAVE A BAD PERSONALITY

No one will believe you're a Technology Prima Donna unless you have a personality so unpleasant that your dog stuffs Gravy Train in his ears whenever you're near. Make it clear to those who would impose on you that there is a price to pay to be in your presence, and that price is exposure to your personality.

The Technology Prima Donna's Golden Rule

Anyone who asks a question is a moron.
The people who don't ask questions are morons too.

As a Technology Prima Donna, you have the right to look down on the ignorant masses who don't have your technical brilliance. But it's not sufficient to merely think contemptuous thoughts about others. You must let them know what you are thinking, through words and actions.

User: I have a technical problem.

Prima Donna: That figures.

User:	I can't print, for some reason.
Prima Donna	I think I know the reason, but I'd have to x-ray your head to be sure.
User:	I think it's a software conflict.
Prima Donna:	Pffft (said with spittle).

NEVER RESPOND TO QUESTIONS

The only downside to being a Technology Prima Donna is that your co-workers will continually ask you questions. If you give simple and helpful answers, that will only encourage more questions. And if you admit you don't know the answers, that will blow your cover as a Technology Prima Donna. Your best bet is to avoid giving any answer at all. There are two good ways to do that. The first way is to simply ignore the people who ask the questions, as if they don't exist. Most people will repeat the question, louder each time, until finally giving up. As the defeated person turns to leave in anger, say, "It depends." That makes it seem as though you weren't ignoring the person, you were only thinking hard about the question. Most people will give up at this point, realizing that a conversation with you could take months. That's just enough effort on your part to protect you against accusations of unhelpfulness.

The second way to avoid giving answers is to tell people to reboot their system, no matter what the problem is. That rarely works, but it buys you time to escape. Look at your pager and mutter "Uh-oh," then walk briskly to your nearest hideout. In all likelihood, the user's problem will be solved before you can be located.

DRESS LIKE A BLIND HOBO

Your dedication to looking unattractive is the most reliable indicator that you have godlike technical skills. The Technology Prima Donna's wardrobe should look like it were stolen from a blind hobo, who, despite being visually challenged, put up a mighty struggle as he was being stripped.

Say yes to facial hair, but only the scraggly kind. If you're capable of growing a thick, attractive beard, you'll have to pluck out some in-between hairs to get the look you need. If you're female, you'll have to harvest some hair from elsewhere (don't make me say it) and glue it to your chin.

The hair on top of your head, if you have any, should be a mirror image of your chin. If you match your eyebrows to your mustache, you have a good chance of looking the same if turned upside down. That can come in handy. For example, if you drop a pen, and you're bending down to pick it up just as someone comes up behind you, you can look from between your legs and freak him out.

YELL WITHOUT PROVOCATION

As a Technology Prima Donna, you don't need a reason to yell. Nor does it matter if you're yelling at anyone in particular. Your anger at the slightest imperfection in others is a sure sign that you have high standards. (Double standards, but high nonetheless.) There are two types of yelling, both worth doing. The first kind is the "crazy street person" yell that is not directed at anyone nearby. It should be loud enough that people throughout your department can enjoy it, and obscene enough to show how passionate you are about your work. Let one fly periodically whether you're angry or not.

The second kind of yelling is the "I might hit you" yell that is so effective in meetings. Normal employees would be fired for verbally abusing a co-worker or vendor, but you are not normal. As a Technology Prima Donna, you have every right to rise out of your chair, scrunch your face up in a pained expression, and insult anyone who has disappointed you. Vendors are the easiest targets, because they won't fight back. But you can attack co-workers too, as long as you include in your rant something about "the benefit of the stockholders." It's the stockholder reference that distinguishes the Technology Prima Donna from ordinary suspected serial killers.

BE MYSTERIOUS AND ECCENTRIC

Leave ambiguous clues about your wild and dangerous lifestyle. Put motorcycle keys on your desk where people will see them, even if you don't own a motorcycle. Dress entirely in leather at least one day per month. If another motorcycle enthusiast asks what kind of bike you ride, ask him to first tell you what he rides. When he does, just mutter, "Lawnmower." Then walk away.

Drape an empty gun holster over your guest chair. If anyone asks where the gun is, say, "Depends. Whose side are you on?" That will give you a reputation as a mysterious and dangerous player.

All Technology Prima Donnas have eccentric hobbies, like ostrich wrestling, or dung sculpture, or playing bridge. Invent an odd hobby for yourself and leave early one day a week to pursue it. Odd hobbies are a sign of brilliance, so it further reinforces your mystique.

DON'T RETURN PHONE CALLS

Technology Prima Donnas are much too busy to return phone calls. If you make the mistake of returning a call, you will seem accessible and underworked. Those are the wrong signals to send. Soon, more people will call you and try to make you work. Returning phone calls is a no-win situation. If you must return a call, do it when you know the person is not there, and leave a message without your return phone number, in case the person has already lost it.

A good way to avoid phone conversations is to have your voice-mail greeting tell callers they can only reach you by paging you. It's more credible to claim you didn't get a page than a voice-mail. You might need that extra level of deniability in case you get cornered in the cafeteria by the victim of your ignorement.

MUMBLE UNINTELLIGIBLY DURING MEETINGS

There are two types of communication that sound exactly the same to your co-workers: (1) nonsense, and (2) highly intelligent stuff. No one will suspect you of speaking nonsense if you remember to look down your nose at people when you talk. Your co-workers will sit quietly and listen, feeling increasingly stupid for not understanding a word you say. To increase the discomfort of your co-workers, mumble. They'll not only feel dense, they'll also feel as though they're going deaf. If anyone insists that you speak up, yell. Try to avoid any volume in between the extremes.

DRAW ABSURDLY COMPLICATED DIAGRAMS ON WHITEBOARDS

Diagrams are the physical equivalent of mumbling. If you are forced to write anything down, make sure it's on a whiteboard where it cannot easily be saved or duplicated. And make sure it's absurdly complicated. Your diagrams should be bristling with lines and boxes and acronyms, the type of markings you might find on an advanced alien spacecraft. Don't restrict yourself to the normal human alphabet. Invent new letters and sprinkle them in the mix. If anyone questions it, explain that some ideas are too big for the alphabet. At night, sneak into the office where you wrote on the whiteboard and erase everything. The janitor will take the rap.

COMPLAIN

You're not a Technology Prima Donna unless you're complaining about something. It will take some practice, but you can train yourself to hate everything in your immediate environment, plus all of the things you've read about in magazines. If a co-worker mentions a new technology, launch into a lengthy harangue about its inherent limitations and lack of backward compatibility. One of the marks of a genuine Technology Prima Donna, ironically, is an obsessive preference for old technology. Any mention of replacing your existing systems with new systems should be met with the sort of scorn normally reserved for war criminals and Congress.

INTERVIEWING FOR FUN

In many fields, especially in technology areas, there are more jobs than there are qualified candidates. If you're a qualified candidate with highly sought-after skills, take advantage of the opportunity to go on interviews just for fun. It's your chance to act like a minor celebrity. There are few things more enjoyable than sitting in a comfortable chair, wearing your nicest clothes, eating doughnuts, and listening to some stranger tell you how talented and valuable you are.

Once you're full of pastries and beverages, start making impossible demands of your prospective employer. Ask if the company will provide twenty-four-hour bodyguards for you. Refuse to explain why you think you need one. Ask for a company car. If you get the car, ask if the interviewer would agree to be your driver. Make ridiculous salary demands based on comparisons to other industries.

"Travolta gets twenty million per movie. I'm thinking of something in that range."

Eventually your prospective employer will realize it's hopeless and end the interview. But not before giving you some free stuff, like a cool jackknife with his company's name on it, or possibly a desk clock. These make excellent gifts for co-workers. Ask to have them gift-wrapped.

▶ THE JOY OF CREATING LOVELY DOCUMENTS

If you work in a cubicle, it's hard to get any satisfaction from your accomplishments. Generally speaking, your work gets combined with the work of other people until your contribution is diluted or deleted. And because your contribution to the company often has no physical dimensions, you rarely get a chance to step back and admire the beauty of your work. That's where the joy of creating lovely documents comes into play.

If your job requires you to create documents or presentations, this can be a source of great job satisfaction. Early in your career you might have been under the impression that documents are just a means to an end. Eventually you figure out that the "ends" are enjoyed by the stockholders, not you. You must find a way to get joy from the means, because that's the only part of the process you'll experience. Solution: Create lovely documents.

You can spend your entire day creating a Powerpoint presentation that has no significance to the world, yet it brings you great personal satisfaction. I used to enjoy printing out my Powerpoint slides and just staring at them, reveling at the beauty of the layout and the clarity of the words. No one else got any joy out of my Powerpoint slides. Often they weren't even used because the meetings got canceled. But communicating information wasn't the point. It was all about beauty. Powerpoint slides are like children, in the sense that no matter how ugly they are, you'll think they are beautiful if they belong to you.

The best part of making lovely documents is that not only does it *look* like work, it *is* work! It's just as fun—and just as unproductive—as avoiding work, but it carries no risk. If your boss sees you spending the entire morning pasting clip art of animals and clouds into your worthless-but-beautiful Powerpoint slides, you might even get some sort of employee award.

▶ THE JOY OF SARCASM

Sarcasm can get you fired if your boss realizes you aren't being a team player. But that risk is low. Your sarcasm will go safely undetected if you simply use your boss's own words. This is obviously the easiest form of sarcasm to master, since it requires no creativity. It doesn't even have to make sense.

The difference between sarcasm and sucking up is a subtle one. In both cases you're thinking to yourself, "I am a lying weasel." Only your facial expressions are different. Suck-ups tend to look like cult members, with those big dopey eyes that say, "Thank you for taking all of my assets." Sarcasm requires the practitioner to appear earnest but not brainwashed. This can be achieved with a variation of the poker face that I call the "pucker face."

The look of earnestness is controlled primarily by two parts of your face: Your lips and the little wrinkly space between your eyebrows. (Note: If you're one of those people who have one long eyebrow, shave a hole in the middle so your wrinkly part will show.)

Never laugh when you're being sarcastic. It will ruin the effect. If you feel the uncontrollable need to giggle, wait until your boss says something hilarious, such as, "Is this only Wednesday? It feels like Friday already!" Then you can throw back your head, open your mouth like you're about to swallow a live porpoise, and laugh like a naked teenager in a field full of pussy willows. Sincerity like that will make your sarcasm all the more convincing.

When you're being sarcastic, remember to smile, but not a normal smile. The lips should be distended slightly from the gums. It's part pucker, part grin. To everyone except your boss, the pucker-smile is a thousand-watt beacon that says, "I am being a wise-ass now."

Sarcasm is best in person, but it also works well in writing, as the e-mail message below clearly shows. Because it's written, not spoken, the pucker technique is different: Notice how the letter "m" is typed with a slight pucker and the letter "I" has a slight wrinkle over it.*

From: [name withheld]
To: scottadams@aol.com

I thought that you would be interested in another verification of your office viewpoint and how Wally's weekly activity report got into my employment record. After seeing it in one of the daily strips, it seemed perfect for a slot in my annual performance review. So I copied Wally's line, "I streamlined my business processes while honing my participatory style and my proactive attitude, all while valuing diversity," into my description of work in the review. My pointy-haired boss either didn't see the humor in it or didn't read it at all and it is now part of my permanent record as an employee.

*Made you look.

There's a fine line between subtle, professional sarcasm and its cousin, total bull. But both have a valuable place in the business world. Here's an example of someone who crossed the line but still got good results.

From: [name withheld]
To: scottadams@aol.com

Recognizing that there are idiots out there who actually embrace Quality and all it entails, I had to give a Quality briefing the other day.

I know nothing about quality and, frankly, couldn't care less. I made up some slides (Powerpoint, of course) and just wrote what I considered absolute nonsense. I actually pulled suggestions from your book *(The Dilbert Principle)* and inserted buzzwords. The sentences themselves had no meaning that I could discern. I spoke for thirty minutes and said nothing.

I was hailed as having the best presentation that day.

Another good way to avoid punishment for sarcasm is to reword your boss's ridiculous advice into the form that most clearly shows its complete lack of value. Then continue to support the ridiculous advice as though it made perfect sense to you, as in this example.

Sarcasm need not be limited to your boss. Your co-workers are acceptable targets too. The only difference is that your co-workers will realize you're being a wise-ass and seek revenge later. But it's often worth it.

5

Office Pranks

I once worked with a guy who said he wished flies were larger so he could hear them yell when he killed them with a fly swatter. To me, this seemed like a dangerous wish, because you never know when your wish might instantly come true. Imagine how mad you'd be if you spent your one magical wish on fly enlargement. Big flies might be less fun than you think. You'd need a tennis racket to bring one down. If you hit one, there'd be tentacles and fly pieces everywhere. You'd have to burn your clothes and move to a new house every time you swatted one.

And what if you didn't specify how much larger you wished the flies to be? An unspecified wish could get you in trouble. If the flies were too big—say the size of a German shepherd—I'll bet there would be legislation to protect them. They'd be big enough to rip the roof off your house and clean out your pantry while you were at work. Life's hard enough without being attacked by giant doglike flies who have legal immunity.

All things considered, it's probably a good thing that flies are small. And since they are, you'll have to look elsewhere to find satisfying screams of horror. I recommend looking to your co-workers. They're bigger than flies, just as annoying, and always willing to let out a good yelp if the situation calls for it. And there's no legislation against any of the things I'm suggesting, as far as I know. But I must admit I've never read any legislation.

Pranks have a long tradition in the workplace. You can use

them to stimulate creativity, reduce stress, and increase team-work. Or you can use them to humiliate your co-workers in a way that will haunt them for the rest of their mortal existence. Whatever.

Below I have compiled some of the best pranks I have collected from *Dilbert* readers. Use them at your own risk. Most of them will get you fired or beaten.

According to my readers, most *Dilbert* books are enjoyed from the privacy of the "home library" (you know what I mean). You might want to bookmark the following section and save it for that purpose. The prank section is ideally suited for that purpose, because each one is like a little story in its own right.

FAMILY RESEMBLANCE PRANK

Borrow the family photos from your co-worker's desk. Scan them into your computer. Use Photoshop software to replace the faces of family members with your own face. Print your doctored photo on a color printer, put them in the picture frames, and return them to their original place. There are many variations on this prank. For example, if the victim is a married man, replace the face of just one of his children with yours.

RAT DROPPINGS

Start a rumor that a rat has been seen in the office. Get a bag of chocolate sprinkles, the kind used for ice cream. Leave some chocolate sprinkles on your victim's desk, next to some paper that appears to have been gnawed. Tape a toy mouse to your victim's phone receiver, but tucked under so it can't be seen easily. When your victim enters his cubicle and sees the droppings, before he can examine them carefully, call his number.

SOUPED-UP PC

Convince a co-worker that you know a trick for improving PC performance. Explain how you can prop a small book under the back of the PC so the electricity can run downhill on its way to the keyboard. Act like you see a definite difference. Encourage him to share the secret with others.

SECRET MESSAGE

Write a secret message on a blank piece of paper and slip it into the paper tray of the office photocopier, a few sheets down. The next person who makes copies will get your message on his document.

This prank is very flexible. For example, you could write a message in the margin professing love for the recipient of the document and suggesting a rendezvous later. Don't spare the adjectives.

Or your message could look like a margin scrawl that was put there by the vice president of your area—something like, "I never realized how incompetent your co-workers were. Thanks for having the courage to name names.—Jerry."

A variation on this prank is to create a fake organization chart and label it "Proposed Organization." Make sure you give the most heinous morons the best positions. Leave it in the copier's paper tray upside down, so it ends up on the back of someone's document. Another variation is to use a proposed cubicle seating diagram instead of an organization chart.

CAKE IQ TEST

For your next office celebration, frost and decorate a shirt box. Add candles. Do the song. Clap. Give the person of honor a dull knife and ask him to cut the cake. See how long it takes him to figure out he's sawing on a piece of cardboard. Take bets and use a stopwatch to determine the winner.

It's a good idea to have the real cake nearby, since the person you are humiliating will be armed with a dull knife.

PHONE WIRE PRANK

This classic phone prank has been around for years. Call your victim and say you're the phone company and you need his help. Explain that there is too much wire from his line in the central office of the phone company. Ask him to pull the wire on his end to take up the slack. If he does it, encourage him to pull harder because it doesn't seem to be working. You can get some people to yank the wire right out of the wall.

PHONE-CLEANING PRANK

From: [name withheld]
To: scottadams@aol.com

For April Fool's Day I talked our IS department into sending out the following e-mail to the company. It was inspired by the Dilbert Newsletter.

"This weekend the company will be doing a network upgrade and tonight we will be doing some simple maintenance of the company phone system. Shortly after midnight the phone company will be blowing the static from the phone lines to enable better reception. In order to ensure a constant pressure we are asking you to cover your phone receiver and headset in a static bag. You can pick up your static bags from (name) at the IS help desk. The procedure should take about one hour and you may remove the bags in the morning."

About twelve people rushed around looking for the bags and dutifully covered their phones. That night we put shredded paper, lint, and cans in the bags to show them what got "blown" out.

PHONE TONE PRANK

Yet another ageless prank: Call your victim and say you're a line tester for the phone company. Explain that there have been reports of static from other users in your area. Ask the user to whistle the "Star-Spangled Banner" while you run some sound tests on your end. Tell the victim to keep it up until you give the word, otherwise the tests will be useless and you'll have to redo them. Put the phone down and go to lunch.

MICROWAVE PRANK

Put an official Microwave Tracking Form next to the microwave. The form should be both illogical and useless. See how many people put their names on it. Here's an example. Modify it to suit your need.

Microwave Tracking Form

Please help us determine the ideal warm-up times for this microwave oven. Record the length of time you let it warm up before putting your food in. Standard warm-up times are anywhere from 1 to 4 minutes.

Employee	Describe Food	Warm-Up Time
_____	_____	_____
_____	_____	_____
_____	_____	_____
_____	_____	_____

FIRST IMPRESSIONS

Walk up to any two co-workers, let's call them Joe and Bob, and say, "Hey, Joe, do your impression of Bob!" When Joe protests that he doesn't do an impression of Bob, say, "Don't be modest. You had the whole room howling yesterday." Then turn and leave.

MOOCH PRANK

This prank is designed for the office mooch who always wants to eat your goodies. Buy a bag of licorice. Open one end of the hollow licorice and fill it with salt. Wait for the office mooch to ask for a piece. Don't do this in your own cubicle, because there's a good chance there will be some spitting and flailing.

MONITOR UPGRADE

When your computer-illiterate co-worker tries to upgrade from Windows 95 to Windows 98, inform him that it requires a new video monitor. Mumble something about the "video drivers" and shake your head with disgust. When your victim puts in a requisition for a new monitor, and it comes back to him covered with laugh-spittle, say, "I guess they patched that bug."

TELEPHONE SHOUTER

This prank works best with co-conspirators. Have several people call the victim under various pretenses. Ask the victim to talk louder because you can't hear him well. If he offers to call you back, just repeat the process. See how loud you can get him to shout.

This prank has the advantage that it annoys not only your victim but all the people in his vicinity.

ASBESTOS WARNING

From: [name withheld]
To: scottadams@aol.com

Here's a good one. Someone mailed a petri dish and one denture-cleaning tablet to a co-worker, with an official memo that explained it was a test for asbestos in the office environment.

The memo directed "all employees" to conduct a simple test: Fill the petri dish with water and drop the tablet in. If the water turns blue, there is asbestos in your office and you must leave immediately.

Dozens of people were standing out on the street, befuddled, bemused, and completely had.

CAR KEYS

From: [name withheld]
To: scottadams@aol.com

When one of my office mates went out to lunch and left his keys on his desk, I went to lunch and made a copy of his car keys. For the next three months I would do little stuff to his car—turn it around, move it over a couple spaces or a couple rows, very subtle things. The one thing not so subtle I did almost every day was to reset all the preset buttons on his radio to the local elevator-music channel. For three months the guy didn't say a word about it to anyone. Finally, at my going-away party, I walked up to him, removed his key from my key chain, and handed it to him. It was very amusing to see the lights come on. I felt really bad when he told me he took his car into the dealership four times in futile attempts to get his radio fixed.

E-MAIL TO ALL

From: [name withheld]
To: scottadams@aol.com

In our group, we have group e-mail lists, some that contain the e-mail addresses of everybody in our group.

A co-worker and myself have been trading rather nasty jokes by e-mail for several weeks and one day he sent me the nastiest of all nasty jokes.

So I replied to him with the e-mail he sent me—but I edited the address headers to look like he had sent it out to the entire group and not just me. I asked him if he intended to send it to the whole group!

Well, I think that just about ruined his whole day. I walked by his cubicle and he was pretty frantic. He told me that he couldn't believe that he could make such a mistake. He asked me if there was a way to recall it from the group. I looked at his panicked condition and just couldn't keep my face straight.

IF YOU BUILD IT, THEY WILL COME

From: [name withheld]
To: scottadams@aol.com

Shortly after we installed new workstations on every faculty desk throughout the department, I discovered it was easy to launch applications remotely on my colleagues' machines. I created a program to play a sound at random times, particularly early evenings. I then recorded an urgent whisper, "Hey, Joe! Over here!" I launched the application using that sound file on Joe's machine. The amusement lasted for weeks!

ANAL-RETENTIVE PRANK

From: [name withheld]
To: scottadams@aol.com

I once had a terribly oppressive, controlling boss. He was an anal-retentive attorney, with every pleat pressed, extra starch in his collars, his shoes shined just so.

So on days that he gave me a hard time, I would sit at my desk and toss a single paper clip on the carpet just outside his door. It never failed—he'd open his door and before he could go any farther, he had to hitch up his pants legs a little by pinching them exactly on the pleats, bend over, and pick up the paper clip. Then he'd place it carefully in the paper-clip holder on my desk.

It seemed like he'd get a clue, when I'd do this sometimes 3–4 times a day, but nope.

I used to imagine what would happen if he, say, broke both legs so he couldn't bend over to pick up the paper clip. I bet he'd still be circling around in front of that office door, unable to proceed farther.

BEWARE OF YOUR COMPUTER

If you can get password access to a co-worker's computer, the opportunities for pranks are limitless.

From: [name withheld]
To: scottadams@aol.com

I work in the MIS department of a small firm, which pretty much gives me access to anyone's computer here to do upgrades, fixes, etc. I also had a co-worker who was constantly pulling little pranks on me. It got to the point where it was really annoying.

One day I found a neat little Macintosh extension that allows you to send messages to another Mac user so that it looks just like a system error. I installed it on her computer and one day before lunch set it off with the following message:

"The Radiation Shield of your monitor has failed!! Please move away from the computer as fast as you can."

There was a loud screech and my co-worker came running out of her cubicle, to the laughter of many witnesses.

Revenge . . . oh, how sweet it is.

Note: If someone writes another prank program of that sort, a nice touch would be to make the entire screen distort slightly as if from the radiation leak.

SPEED 3—THE COMPUTER

A variant on the prank above is to send error messages to your victim's computer saying he must press a key every five seconds to avoid a hard disk crash. Show a countdown on screen that resets after any keystroke. See how long you can get your victim to sit there pressing the key. When your victim yells for help, offer to find someone who knows how to fix that exact problem. Then leave for the day.

GOD IS TALKING TO YOU

From: [name withheld]
To: scottadams@aol.com

I was able to gain control of my boss's computer through the network. I opened up WordPerfect on her computer and typed, "Come into the light." Upon reflection, this may have been a little mean, but I still remember not being able to breathe due to my laughter after she told me that God had revealed to her that he was coming for her.

SPOOGE BUCKET

From: [name withheld]
To: scottadams@aol.com

The engineering department was on a floor that had no plumbing. So, instead of walking all the way downstairs to spill out old coffee, pop, etc., we put a huge white bucket (commonly referred to as "the spooge bucket") in the furnace room, and disposed of our various unwanted liquids there.

Normally, the spooge bucket was emptied once a week, but in this instance, maintenance must have forgotten about it and the bucket got excessively full. So full, in fact, that the only things retaining some of the liquid were the law of surface tension and the nice healthy layer of white mold growing over the entire top.

Well, on her first day, our brand-new co-worker needed to spill out her cold coffee and asked where she could do so. One of the enterprising young engineers told her that she could dump it in the "covered bucket" in the furnace room. A minute or so later, a shriek of disgust echoed down the hallway as she plunged her hand into the "lid" to remove it.

I'M WATCHING

From: [name withheld]
To: scottadams@aol.com

Our company does remote video applications. I told some-one in our accounting group (who was delaying a number of my expense payments) that I had downloaded a new mouse driver to her PC that allowed me to use her mouse as a camera and microphone. I explained that I did not appreciate what she had recently said and done with my expense paperwork. My expense reports used to take up to two months to get paid, now it happens in days.

Note: A variation of this prank is to tell people that the new computer monitors have built-in video cameras and microphones

so employees can be watched through the local network by anyone who has the right software.

ADD A MEG TO YOUR PC

From: [name withheld]
To: scottadams@aol.com

I came to work early and discovered that one of our VPs
had left his notebook computer on all night with absolutely
no password protection.

I located a sound file, the one where Meg Ryan is doing
that fake orgasm in *When Harry Met Sally*, and installed it
on this VP's PC. I assigned this sound to every single
Windows event so there would be virtually nothing he
could do without exciting Meg.

For good measure, I also cranked the volume on his PC to
maximum, gambling on the probability that he would be so
flustered, he wouldn't be able to find the volume control.

When teaching someone a lesson, it is vitally important
that other people are present so they learn by example.
These are called witnesses, and I had lots.

When the VP triggered the sound for the first time, we
were on the floor with laughter. He didn't know how to
make the sound stop. Shutting the door to his office didn't
help much. The sound still carried halfway through the

building, attracting many more witnesses than I had originally invited.

Forty-five minutes later and after countless attempts (he never found the volume control), the VP finally removed the last of the Meg Ryan sounds.

That night, the VP took his notebook home. Lesson learned.

UPSIDE-DOWN MONITOR

From: [name withheld]
To: scottadams@aol.com

One day while browsing the Web I came upon a font that looks like regular letters except everything is upside down.

I loaded the font onto the computer of a particularly computer-illiterate co-worker and changed the settings so that font would be used by Windows for everything.

I left a note for our tech support guy explaining the prank. When my victim called tech support about his sudden problem, he was told that it would be necessary to order a new part. In the meantime he could try turning his computer monitor upside down.

He was in the process of flipping his monitor over when I stopped by.

POSSESSED ANSWERING MACHINE

From: [name withheld]
To: scottadams@aol.com

There was a particularly annoying employee we wanted to put in her place. We phoned her home during the work-day, and when her answering machine answered, we conferenced the call to her work number. Needless to say, she was COMPLETELY FREAKED OUT that her answering machine had CALLED HER AT WORK. Lucky for the three of us involved in the prank, we were able to keep straight faces as she explained what had happened—and even suggested that perhaps her answering machine was possessed. I wonder if she ever figured it out.

LOW BATTERY

From: [name withheld]
To: scottadams@aol.com

If your target carries an alphanumeric pager, send him repetitive pages, with the message, "Low battery."

Be sure your paging terminal does not automatically add a signature or date code to the page.

The victim will constantly change his pager battery or, better, will send the pager to the repair depot only to have it returned with, "No problem found." That's when you start sending the "low battery" pages again.

Many alpha paging systems can now be accessed from the Web, which makes it easy for you to perform this prank while appearing to do your job.

HUBCAPS

From: [name withheld]
To: scottadams@aol.com

One of my co-workers lost two hubcaps off his car; he drove around for months like this. One day we removed the two remaining hubcaps and took them up to his office.

I told him that a friend of mine was scrapping a car just like his, so I grabbed two hubcaps off it before it went to the wreckers. I handed them to my co-worker for his car.

(My accomplices felt I should have won an Oscar for keeping a straight face throughout this.)

He looked at the two hubcaps and noted how they were EXACTLY the same as his; they even had similar dings and scratches!

Later at lunch he took the two "new" hubcaps out to his car. He noticed that the other hubcaps were missing and said, "Oh, man, you should have gotten me four!"

PAINTED FINGERNAILS

From: [name withheld]
To: scottadams@aol.com

We used to do this at a company where I worked a few
years ago. When people stand in a co-worker's cubicle,
they sometimes rest their hand on the top of the cubicle
wall. If you happened to be in the next cubicle, you could
easily paint a large dot on each of their fingernails with
White-Out.

PHONE FROM HELL

From: [name withheld]
To: scottadams@aol.com

We used to entertain ourselves by going into someone's
office and taping down the off-hook button on the phone.
Then we would call the person and watch the reaction
when the phone doesn't stop ringing after the receiver is
picked up.

We used to get one guy this way at least once a week.

FREE MONEY

From: [name withheld]
To: scottadams@aol.com

We have an annual Christmas-tree lighting event hosted by our CEO. The event is optional and typically only a small fraction of our workforce shows up. Some of us decided to play a trick on those who don't go to this heartwarming event. We all went to our banks and got crisp new $100 bills. After the tree-lighting event we went back to the office showing off our $100 bills that we "were given" at the tree-lighting ceremony. I think the attendance will go up this year.

BLEEP YOU

From: [name withheld]
To: scottadams@aol.com

I wrote a little Visual Basic program that would emit a single beep at random intervals between 17 and 22 minutes. I installed it on the PC of the guy in the cubicle next to mine. I put it in his C:\Windows\System directory and set it to run automatically. The key to keeping a prank file unnoticed is to give it an official-sounding name, like dev-sup32.exe. The randomness of the beep makes it all the more difficult to troubleshoot.

The best part of this prank is that I'm learning all kinds of new words. He usually says something like, "What the heck is that?" But the word "heck" is replaced with something more vulgar.

PHONE YANK

From: [name withheld]
To: scottadams@aol.com

Use a pipe cleaner to tie the receiver cord of a phone to itself, effectively making it very short. When the phone rings, your victim will jerk the entire phone off the desk.

Note: This is especially useful when having meetings with rude co-workers who answer their phone while you're in their office.

PRESUMED DEAD

From: [name withheld]
To: scottadams@aol.com

I used to work with someone who read his (paper) mail only once in a while. He would let it pile up in his in-box until no more would fit, then he'd go through it all at once.

One day, while he was out of the office, a colleague of his took the whole pile from the in-box, wrote "DECEASED" on each piece, and put all the mail in his out-box.

He told me that it took the better part of a year to sort out the resulting mess.

AIR RAID

From: [name withheld]
To: scottadams@aol.com

The burglar alarm in our facility had a test switch, allowing the system to emit a screeching howl. When my co-workers arrived, my manager and I explained that the company required us to have an air-raid drill in case of nuclear attack. Our co-workers, all young, thought that this was stupid, but they believed that the word had come down from on high to stage an air-raid drill.

We explained that when they heard the alarm, the cashiers should all pull out their registers, run to safety zones, and SHIELD THE CASH WITH THEIR BODIES. The drill went off according to training.

A few days later, they were less than amused when we let them in on our little prank.

PEANUTS FROM HEAVEN

From: [name withheld]
To: scottadams@aol.com

On the night before my last day at a job, I spent hours constructing a delicate setup. When my boss came in the next morning, while the entire office watched (since I had told of my prank), he sat down in his chair and read a note on his desk asking for a certain document. He leaned over to open his large file drawer. As he opened it, it pulled a wire that went through a series of pulleys, eventually moving a ceiling tile. Above that tile was 27 cubic feet of Styrofoam peanuts, corralled and "aimed" using cardboard that was taped together. The peanuts poured down on my boss for about ten seconds. At the end of this onslaught was a sign that dangled down from the ceiling: "Aren't you glad today's my last day?"

POWER STRIPPING

From: [name withheld]
To: scottadams@aol.com

I used to work with a fellow who loved to play pranks on his supervisor. The supervisor's computer was plugged into a power strip under his desk. Every morning he would crawl under his desk to turn on the power strip.

One night our prankster connected a 110 dB emergency horn to the power strip and hid the horn behind the desk. From three doors down, we heard the horn go off, we heard the supervisor's head hit the underside of the desk, and we heard the supervisor yelling the prankster's name.

SNEEZE SLAP

From: [name withheld]
To: scottadams@aol.com

Fill your hands with water, walk behind one of your co-workers, pretend to sneeze, and throw the water on the back of your co-worker's neck. For extra effect, keep walking, staring at your hands, only murmuring under your breath what an amazing sneeze that was, what great distance you got, and how the soakage factor was extra high.

THRONE PHONE

Run fake wires into restroom stalls, originating from someplace hard to trace. Post notices inside the stalls that phones will be installed so employees can avoid downtime. Act like you think it's a good idea and don't know what all the fuss is about.

BAD TECHNICAL ADVICE

Any form of bad technical advice can be entertaining. Try to make your bad advice the kind that will make your victim do something stupid in front of witnesses. Here are some examples of advice to give someone whose computer keeps locking up:

▶ It might be overheating. Try fanning it with a large binder every ten minutes or so.

▶ Hold your phone up to the computer so I can hear it. Then type rhythmically, like a heartbeat.

▶ Your mouseball might be losing flexibility. Try taking it out of the mouse and massaging it.

▶ Your screen might need a sonic degaussment. Try whistling an E flat at the screen. It takes about a minute to work.

▶ Your computer might be picking up interference from CB radio users in the area. Try yelling into the computer, "Please switch to another frequency! Over."

▶ It's a static electricity problem. Remove your shoes and socks when typing. And don't let the keyboard get near any other clothing. Hitch your chair way back and reach forward to the keyboard when using it.

▶ I've been hearing about this problem lately. It's caused by the upcoming solar eclipse. Try putting a pinhole in a shoe box and viewing your screen through it.

▶ To properly ground yourself when the PC case is open, use an antistatic wrist clip. If none is handy, you can use a regular dog leash. Put the collar on yourself and attach the leash to the side of the PC case using a large paper clip.

You can avoid retribution for your bad advice by stating it in the form of a question. That way you don't have to take responsibility when things go terribly wrong. You can say, "Hey, I was only asking." Here are some good questions to ask your PC-illiterate co-workers.

▶ Have you tried picking it up and shaking it?

▶ Did you ever think of soaking it in vinegar?

▶ I wonder what happens if you run a huge magnet over it?

CUBICLE STOOGE

Let's say a co-worker is desperately trying to concentrate on a vital project that is on deadline—the kind where any distraction is a horrible inconvenience. Call a person in the cubicle adjacent to your victim and ask inane questions, like, "In your budget projections, are you assuming a hundred cents to the dollar?" Insist that you have a bad connection and ask the person to speak louder and louder. Not only will the person to whom you're talking get louder, but he will be angry. Plus he will be saying completely non-sensical things like, "TWO PEOPLE WITH SMALL HEADS ARE NOT THE SAME AS ONE HEADCOUNT!!!"

This will make your victim insanely angry, but not at you. You'll be safe and snug in your cubicle yards away.

WHERE'S THAT OPTION?

Make passing references to how you just used the company's new document management system to save yourself a lot of work. Explain how you routed your printer output to the copy machine and had the documents automatically collated and stapled. Then you sent an e-mail message to the In-house Document Delivery Group (IDDG), who distributed all two hundred copies the same day. If your co-worker asks how to do that, give a vague answer involving an icon on his computer that resembles a "cross between a Mobius strip and a picnic." Your co-worker will spend days looking for that icon on his own computer. Anytime he asks for more specifics, change the subject.

FUN WITH SPEAKERPHONES

If one of the people at your meeting is participating from a remote location via speakerphone, this is a good opportunity to find happiness at his expense, without much risk of retaliation. Take one of the life-size moron masks on the following pages—there's one for each gender—and put it over the speakerphone. Or

look between pages 216 and 217 of this book for your very own punch-out speakerphone masks of the Boss and Alice.

SOUNDS THAT DRIVE CO-WORKERS CRAZY

You can produce sounds in the office that will drive your co-workers insane. That can be very entertaining. Every co-worker is different, so you might have to experiment to find the sounds that are the most annoying to your cubicle neighbor. It's worth the effort.

According to my e-mail, the most annoying sound you can project over a cubicle wall is the sound of clipping your fingernails. Dozens of people have written to me to say that the clip . . . clip . . . clip from the adjoining cubicle is enough to drive them to mayhem. Unfortunately, your fingernails don't grow quickly enough to make this sound as often as you might like. But you can compensate for nature's blunder in that area by recording the sound on your computer and replaying it when you're out.

The list of annoying office noises is long. You can probably invent a few on your own. Here's a starter set to get you going. The criterion for selecting good sounds is that they should be rude, but not so rude that a civilized person will want to make a big deal about it. This delicate balance compounds the effectiveness of the annoyance by adding a little voice to the victim's brain that says over and over, "DOESN'T HE REALIZE HOW RUDE THAT IS?????!!!!"

ANNOYING OFFICE NOISES

► Coffee slurping

► Finger tapping

► Whistling

► Knuckle cracking

► Pen clicking

► All things nasal

COUNTERINTELLIGENCE

It can be fun to fill your co-workers with ridiculous "facts," then wait and see if they repeat them later in front of others. Conceptually, it's a lot like raising carrier pigeons. Both hobbies involve attaching information to creatures with tiny brains, then watching in awe as the information returns days later. There's no real purpose to doing this; it's just amazing that it works.

A good category of ridiculous facts is anything involving world events. Tell a co-worker that you're planning a trip to Alaska, assuming you can get a Russian visa. If your co-worker appears puzzled, explain that the United States recently sold Alaska to Russia after it was learned that the much-vaunted Alaskan oil reserves were only diesel oil after all. This sounds vaguely plausible. If you detect any head-nodding, keep riding that bronco as far as it will take you. Talk wistfully about the old days, when Alaska had its own royal family—the Frozington Dynasty. Tragically, the Frozingtons were all rounded up and executed during the Canadian Wars. Many of the native Alaskans "Esks" were forced into servitude as gardeners in Canada. That's where the derogatory phrase "Esk . . . mow" comes from.

Once the evil seeds are planted, wait about a week and make a passing reference to Alaska in a mixed crowd that includes your victim. Your target will be eager to show off his knowledge of Alaska. This can be very amusing, assuming you avoid laughing so hard that you pass a kidney through your urethra.

Here are some other good "facts" to teach co-workers:

▶ In China, amazingly, no one actually eats Chinese food.

▶ Light travels faster than sound because of the way your ears are shaped.

▶ Spanish is basically the same as French, but with fewer words for cheese.

▶ If a Japanese businessman bows, it means he wants you to rub his head for luck.

▶ Scientists have determined that smoking is okay if you swallow the smoke instead of letting it in your lungs.

▶ If you get an unlisted Social Security number, you don't have to pay taxes.

► You can request copies of your old mail from the post office.

► Every six months, when the earth rotates on its axis, North Korea becomes South Korea and vice versa.

PARANOIA PRANKS

If you know a co-worker who is perpetually paranoid, this trick works well. Take a reusable interoffice envelope—the kind where you cross off the previous address and write in the next on the list—and add two addresses. The victim's name and address should be at the end of the list. The address before the victim's should be Human Resources, or perhaps the legal department, whichever seems scarier in your company. The previous address is the only clue about where the envelope originated from. Tape the envelope closed, mark it "Confidential," then rip it open. Leave the envelope—opened and empty—in the paranoid victim's in-box.

Enlist accomplices to help on the next part. Whenever any of you see the victim, look sincere and say, "Tough break." Or "I don't think you deserved that kind of treatment." Then walk away briskly.

PHONE FUN

If you have at least two co-workers you don't like, that's all you need for phone fun. Sneak into the cubicle of one of them and forward the phone to the other. This is especially effective if they dislike each other as much as you dislike them. Ideally, the two co-workers should be in different buildings or at least on different floors. The person receiving the calls won't be able to call the other victim to sort it out, so they'll have to travel.

A variation on this theme is to call one person, then use the conference-call feature of your phone to call the other. Don't say anything, just connect the two people. Listen to see how long it takes them to figure out neither called the other.

SPEAKERPHONE ABUSERS

The complaint I hear the most about cubicle life is about the idiots who insist on using their speakerphones to conduct business in their cubicles. The resulting noise pollution chokes out productivity in a ten-cubicle radius. You can cure a co-worker of this habit by leaving suggestive messages on the offender's voice-mail system. When the messages are played back, the entire cubicle neighborhood will hear, "Ted, this is Allen from the Sheep Romance Association. Are you thinking of running for treasurer again this year? You've got my vote. In any case, I'll see you at the convention. Wear wool."

Note: Be sure to use an outside line to leave your fake message. Most voice-mail systems transmit the caller's name with the message if you call from a phone on the same system.

FAKE COMPANY POLICIES

Your co-workers have been trained to accept any bizarre company requirement as a matter of course. This gives you great latitude to create your own phony policies to see how many people will believe them.

Employee Organ Donation

Create an Employee Organ Donation form and distribute it to the department. The form should ask for volunteers who wish to have their organs harvested to help defray the expense of providing donuts for company meetings. Include a graph showing the rising cost of pastries. Point out that this is strictly an optional program, although the names of participants will be reported quarterly to the people who make decisions about salaries and promotions.

Employee Dress Code

Create an update to the employee dress code. For realism, make sure it has no basis in common sense. For example, if you already have "casual Friday," you might distribute a memo that introduces "stained Thursday." Stained Thursday would be traditional business clothing, but with slightly relaxed standards for cleanliness, coherence, and odor. It's a transition day to casual Friday. Everyone has at least one great outfit in the closet that has a flaw—a missing button, a permanent stain, a cigarette hole—that sort of thing. Or maybe you're just too lazy to take your outfit to the cleaners, so it smells like a dead giraffe. On stained Thursday those outfits would be considered okay. In your memo, point out that this is the sort of management change that creates winning companies.

Approved Vendor List

Create an "Approved Vendors" list, made up entirely of companies that have gone out of business. Explain in an attached memo that this list has been in development for several years. The new policy requires employees to use the vendors on the list and no others. Find the name of someone who has recently left the company and put that name as the contact person in case there are questions about the policy.

Use What You Sell

Circulate an official-looking e-mail message saying that all employees must use the products your company sells. Suggest that this is a form of punishment for poor performance. If revenues improve next quarter, employees will be allowed to use a competitor's product.

Key Employees

This one is based on a true story: Create a fake policy that says only "key employees" will be allowed to order new business cards. Don't define who the key employees are. This will cause a stampede of people trying to order business cards just to find out if they are "key."

FAXUAL HARASSMENT

Send a fax to a co-worker's regular voice line. Most fax machines will make several attempts to send a fax if it doesn't go through the first time. When your victim answers his phone, he'll get the high-pitched squeal of the fax and realize there is nothing he can do to prevent several more calls just like it. By the fourth call, most victims of this prank will move to a shack in Montana and write a manifesto against technology.

For the more gullible victims, after they complain to you about the repeated calls, tell them to listen carefully to the fax tones because sometimes you can make out the phone number of the calling fax. Explain that fax language is much like human language except more garbled.

MYSTERY MUSIC

Get one of those greeting cards with a music chip that plays an annoying song over and over. Remove the music chip. Sew it into the chair seat of your victim. Or place it above a ceiling tile over the victim's desk. The music should be loud enough to be heard but too faint to be easily located. A similar prank can be performed with a pager instead of a music chip, preferably the victim's pager.

INCREMENTAL INSANITY

This prank has many variations. It involves making slight changes to the placement or dimensions of something in your victim's workspace each day. The changes should be slight enough to avoid immediate detection. For example, lower the height of your victim's chair by one millimeter each day. Eventually the victim will feel he is shrinking. You can compound this feeling by casually mentioning reports you've read lately about how sedentary people get shorter over time. Enlist accomplices to help. Have your accomplices say things like, "Gee, I guess I usually see you wearing higher heels." Or, "That shirt looks a size too big on you."

RESTROOM STALL PRANK

Take an old pair of pants and a pair of shoes and stuff them with newspapers so they appear to be a person's feet as seen from outside the stall. Ideally, match the exact shoe type of your boss. Make a long audio recording of hard-to-identify sounds of ecstasy. The noise should be a random combination of the sounds you make when you . . .

▶ Scratch an itch in the middle of your back.

▶ Taste excellent food.

▶ Have an intense sexual experience.

Feel free to add other unusual sounds—animals screaming, waterfalls, buzzing—depending on how amazingly juvenile and disgusting you are. Put the audiotape in an expensive portable stereo and leave it in the stall with the fake feet. Close the door.

A variation on this prank is to convince a co-worker to pull the prank. Then go in and steal the high-quality stereo. Technically, that's more of a crime than a prank, but it's the kind no one reports.

ANOTHER VERSION OF THE RESTROOM STALL PRANK

From: [name withheld]
To: scottadams@aol.com

One of my co-workers is typically the first in the office each day. One morning, he decided to take a spare pair of men's pants and shoes and place them "appropriately" in one of the stalls of the ladies' rest room.

Many people were quite concerned about this, including one woman who told our HR director, "I think there's a guy in there. But he must be really sick, because he's been in there all morning."

PAVLOVIAN TRAINING FOR CO-WORKERS

You can train your co-workers in the same way Pavlov trained his dogs. It's not immediately obvious why you would want to do this, but it sure is fun, as this report shows.

From: [name withheld]
To: scottadams@aol.com

I work as a security guard. One day, I came back from patrol about five minutes earlier than usual. The guard who watches the doors asked me suspiciously why I had come back early, and accused me of not completing my patrol. She even called our supervisor and complained to him.

I figured that she had a lot of extra time on her hands, so I decided to help her fill some of it.

Her job was to watch the doors and buzz people in with her little access control button. The buzzer is very loud and irritating. There are also access buttons in the security center, where I was stationed. So I pressed the button, just to annoy her. She called me immediately and asked if someone was pressing the button. I innocently told her no. She asked if I knew how she could stop the buzzing. I told her that maybe she should try opening and closing the doors. I watched her on the video monitor as she opened and closed the doors. I stopped the buzzing each time, to convince her that she had discovered the problem. Then I waited and buzzed again. Each time she got up and repeated the successful maneuver.

She never did catch on. She just kept opening the doors and acting all smug that she knew the solution to the problem. But everyone else knew exactly what was going on, and I'm afraid she didn't look like the brightest bulb in the hallway.

INVENTING STRANGE MORALE BOOSTERS

If you've heard of any bizarre and annoying practices at other companies, convince your boss to try it at yours. Better yet, make up a bizarre and annoying practice and tell your boss that it's commonly used in all the *Fortune* 500 companies. I think the poor company below was a victim of just such a prank.

From: [name withheld]
To: scottadams@aol.com

Last week, I received an e-mail message from our highest middle manager in the department. The message explained that, in an attempt to raise morale, the workers would be given an opportunity to play in a "game." To play the game, we all received bright yellow happy faces with our names on them. The purpose of the game was to hold on to the happy face for the duration of one month. Whoever succeeded in doing so would get eight hours extra paid time off.

There's a catch. You lose your happy face if you are ever caught doing something that is construed as a "Non-Positive Attitude." There's no definition of what exactly is a Non-Positive Attitude (NPA). That judgment will be made by what the designers call the "Positivity Police." The Positivity Police are chosen from among the employees by picking names out of a hat. Their job is to report NPA activity to the management.

Once chosen, the e-mail explained, the Positivity Police would reveal their identities only to management.

The funniest part was that no member of the management staff could understand how this could have a negative effect on our attitudes.

MONITORING YOUR CO-WORKERS

If your co-workers are not pulling their weight, and yours too, it might be necessary to measure and report on their performance. This can be a valuable motivator.

From: [name withheld]
To: scottadams@aol.com

A couple of my co-workers would consistently take long breaks and leave early. So another co-worker and I wrote a program that would track the amount of time actually worked compared to time taken for breaks, for each person. The program also allowed us to remotely control their computers. When the person logged on in the morning, a message would appear notifying them of their log-in time. Messages would then appear throughout the day letting them know their work-to-break ratio. If they did not actually work enough hours in a day, when they tried to log off at the end of the day it would not allow them to log off. If they shut off their machines, they would not be allowed to log in the next day (very frustrating).

The Helpdesk could not figure out how the program was working and how to remove it from the computers. A chart report would be generated at the end of each week to show their work and break status. Inevitably, the breaks would add up to almost the same as their actual work.

Surviving Meetings

Unless you work alone, one of the biggest assaults on your happiness is something called a meeting. A meeting is essentially a group of people staring at visual aids until the electrochemical activity in their brains ceases, at which point decisions are made. It's like being in suspended animation, except that people in suspended animation aren't in severe physical discomfort and praying for death.

If you attend many meetings, your life will disappear faster than a bag of cash falling off the back of an armored car in front of a homeless shelter for Olympic sprinters. But not everyone feels bored at meetings. The exception to this rule is the people who have such bad personal lives that they use meetings as a substitute for actual social interactions. Avoid these people if you can:

If you absolutely can't avoid meetings, learn how to enjoy them. Your body might have to sit motionless for hours, but you can train your brain to disengage and enjoy itself.

▶ PERSONAL DIGITAL ASSISTANTS

If your co-workers are bringing PalmPilots and other personal digital assistants (PDAs) to meetings, get a Nintendo Gameboy and try to blend in with the crowd. You might want to paint your Gameboy dark gray and file off the logo. Interrupt the meeting to ask people their phone numbers and addresses. Press buttons randomly on your Gameboy to simulate data entry. If someone offers to transfer his business-card information via infrared signal to your PDA, play along. Point your Gameboy in the appropriate direction, then say, "Got it." When the other person complains that he did not receive your information, recommend that he get his PDA repaired. Once your credibility has been established, through the process of being an unscrupulous weasel, you can merrily play with your Gameboy throughout the meeting.

▶ ROBOT VISUALIZATION

My favorite technique for keeping my brain from burrowing out of my head during meetings is what I call the robot visualization. The way this works is that you imagine your body is a gigantic robot and you are a tiny captain inside it, in the control room. Imagine the control room being like the bridge of the Starship Enterprise. The forward screens are the view out of your eyes. Every movement of your huge robotic body becomes fun that way. You hear your little captain issue the command, "Turn neck thirty degrees starboard." When your neck actually turns, it's very cool. You're the captain of this excellent robot. It's just you in the control room, alone with the attractive and ambitious Ensign Raquel. (Adjust the gender to suit your preferences.) There's no end to the robotic possibilities once the two of you start getting frisky and end up on the weapons control panel.

▶ EMBARRASSING THE PRESENTER

If one of your co-workers is making a presentation, amuse yourself by asking questions that are impossible to answer. Don't limit yourself to questions that make any sense or have any relevance. The objective of this game is to make your co-worker get that "please shoot me" expression in front of a roomful of people. For example, if he is doing a presentation on the budget, ask this sort of question:

"Correct me if I'm wrong, but isn't the depreciation rate a good indication of the declining EVA projection from the perspective of a long-term strategy, vis-à-vis the budget gap?"

When your co-worker's eyes start to look like two pie plates with an olive in the middle of each one, make a dissatisfied face and say, "That's okay. I'll ask someone knowledgeable."

It's also fun to raise issues that will create extra work for the presenter. Compete with the other people at your table to see who can make the presenter work the hardest after the meeting. The key is to look earnest and concerned, so your issue seems impossible to ignore. Here are some good issues that fit almost any situation. Any one of these would require more work than could ever be justified, yet they sound almost important.

ANNOYING ISSUES

"What's the impact on all the other departments in our company? Have you checked with them?"

"How would the numbers look if you did 5 percent less of whatever it is that you were talking about? Could you run those numbers for next week?"

"Maybe you should produce a skit to describe your plan and distribute the videotape throughout the company."

The following story is allegedly true, but sounds more like an urban legend. Either way, it suggests a fun joke to pull on a vendor if you can get your co-workers to collude.

From: [name withheld]
To: scottadams@aol.com

This happened at the headquarters of a large mid-Atlantic bank. A vendor came in to talk about some new software. He set up an overhead projector to use with his computer and asked someone to shut off the lights in the conference room. Everyone just sat there. So he looked around for the light switch but couldn't find it.

Finally someone explained that the company replaced the light switches with motion sensors because people were always leaving the conference-room lights on.

When he asked the employees what they did when they had presentations, they replied that they just "sat real still" until the lights went out.

7

Managing Your Co-Workers

If you're unfortunate enough to have co-workers, you must learn how to manage them. Otherwise, like so many wildebeests on the plains of the Serengeti, they will be bumping into you, drinking from your water hole, and generally kicking up a lot of dust. That will cut into your happiness.

You don't have any official power over co-workers, so you must find other forms of persuasion.

▶ CUBICLE FLATULENCE

According to the e-mail reports I'm getting from the field, cubicle flatulence is a mushrooming problem in corporate America. It might replace secondhand smoke as the biggest menace to public health in the workplace. I'm not aware of any scientific studies on the health dangers of secondhand flatulence, but this is exactly the sort of thing that our universities should be studying. For all we know, people are dropping like flies. But I'm not here to talk about the downside of flatulence. This book is about workplace joy.

Dozens of *Dilbert* readers have mentioned one particular coincidence about cubicle flatulence: It seems to attract visitors.

147

People write to tell me that every time they let one fly, some unsuspecting victim will round the corner and enter their cubicle. This causes a moment of tension, as the visitor, soon aware of the atmospheric disturbance, tries to transact business without the benefit of oxygen. It would be easy to interpret this as a bad situation for all involved. But on more careful observation, it becomes clear that one party in this transaction is getting the benefit of relieved internal pressure and a substantially shorter meeting than would otherwise be the case. It's a classic wind-win situation. The visitor doesn't fare so well. What we can learn from this is that when it comes to flatulence, it's better to give than to receive.

At this writing, I am aware of no companies with written policies forbidding the gassing of co-workers. (You could say it's an open-ended situation.) There might be some international conventions that are applicable, but those are rarely enforced.

▶ BOSSING CO-WORKERS AROUND

Try bossing your co-workers around. Give them assignments; send them to gather information; ask them to work overtime—that sort of thing. Most people will respond with indignation and profanity. But a certain percentage will do exactly as they're told because they're too timid to resist. They might even appreciate the clarity and purpose you have given their lives. Start small, by ordering them to do their own work in ways that will make them look good to their peers. Praise them lavishly for following your orders. Soon they will begin to associate following your orders with pleasant results.

Once you have them conditioned to follow your directions for their own jobs, start to assign some of your work to them. It should be a subtle transition, like asking them to drop things off on the way to other places, or asking them to make copies for you when they are at the copy machine. Slowly expand their assignments to include your core duties. Chastise them for doing their own work before doing yours.

If you have a timid co-worker who vaguely resembles you, give that person a makeover until the two of you are indistinguishable. If you can get someone who looks like you to do your work, you never have to show up at the office again.

▶ BE IN CHARGE OF THE OFFICE MOVE

If your department has to move to new office space, volunteer to be in charge of the move. This will give you absolute power over the future happiness of your co-workers.

During the months leading up to the move, your co-workers will go out of their way to suck up to you. You will live like a cubicle king, meting out punishments and rewards by shuffling the floor layout plan according to who has pleased you lately. Don't worry that taking on this extra duty will keep you from your work. Work is what your serfs are for. They will be glad to pick up your slack in return for a higher priority in the cubicle shuffle.

▶ DEALING WITH IRRATIONAL CO-WORKERS

Nothing can reduce your happiness faster than an argument with an irrational co-worker. You can't win irrational people over to your side by your superior reasoning abilities. And you can't talk them into getting inside abandoned refrigerators and closing the door to see if the light goes out. There simply aren't that many abandoned refrigerators. If you use the refrigerator in the break room, everyone will start whining about how there's no room for yogurt. Until there are more refrigerators, or less yogurt, you will find yourself in frustrating discussions that can have no good endings.

Trying to win an argument with an irrational person is like trying to teach a cat to snorkel by providing written instructions.

No matter how clear your instructions, it won't work. Your best strategy is to reduce the time you spend in that sort of situation.

I have developed a solution to this problem. It is based on the fact that irrational people are easily persuaded by anything that has been published. It doesn't matter who published it, or what the context is, or how inaccurate it is. Once something is published, it's as persuasive as anything else that's ever been published. So I figure that what you need is a publication that supports all of your arguments no matter what they are. This book is that publication.

I have collected the most common arguments made by irrational people into a handy reference guide and titled it "You Are Wrong Because." Circle the irrational arguments that apply to your situation and give a copy to the person who is bugging you. Look smug, as though this were conclusive evidence of your rightness. A rational person might point out that just because something is written down doesn't make it so. But since you're not giving the list to anyone with that much insight, it doesn't really matter. What matters is that you will feel as though you brought closure to a potentially frustrating situation.

You Are Wrong Because

For your convenience, I have circled the brain malfunction(s) that most closely resemble(s) the one(s) you recently made on the topic of (fill in topic): _____.

1. AMAZINGLY BAD ANALOGY

Example: You can train a dog to fetch a stick. Therefore, you can train a potato to dance.

2. FAULTY CAUSE AND EFFECT

Example: On the basis of my observations, wearing huge pants makes you fat.

3. I AM THE WORLD

Example: I don't listen to country music. Therefore, country music is not popular.

4. IGNORING EVERYTHING SCIENCE KNOWS ABOUT THE BRAIN

Example: People choose to be obese/gay/alcoholic because they prefer the lifestyle.

5. THE FEW ARE THE SAME AS THE WHOLE

Example: Some Elbonians are animal rights activists. Some Elbonians wear fur coats. Therefore, Elbonians are hypocrites.

6. GENERALIZING FROM SELF

Example: I'm a liar. Therefore, I don't believe what you're saying.

7. ARGUMENT BY BIZARRE DEFINITION

Example: He's not a criminal. He just does things that are against the law.

8. TOTAL LOGICAL DISCONNECT

Example: I enjoy pasta because my house is made of bricks.

9. JUDGING THINGS WITHOUT COMPARISON TO ALTERNATIVES

Example: I don't invest in U.S. Treasury bills. There's too much risk.

10. ANYTHING YOU DON'T UNDERSTAND IS EASY TO DO

Example: If you have the right tools, how hard could it be to generate nuclear fission at home?

11. IGNORANCE OF STATISTICS

Example: I'm putting ALL of my money on the lottery this week because the jackpot is so big.

12. IGNORING THE DOWNSIDE RISK

Example: I know that bungee jumping could kill me, but it's three seconds of great fun!

13. SUBSTITUTING FAMOUS QUOTES FOR COMMON SENSE

Example: Remember, "All things come to those who wait." So don't bother looking for a job.

14. IRRELEVANT COMPARISONS

Example: A hundred dollars is a good price for a toaster, compared to buying a Ferrari.

15. CIRCULAR REASONING

Example: I'm correct because I'm smarter than you. And I must be smarter than you because I'm correct.

16. INCOMPLETENESS AS PROOF OF DEFECT

Example: Your theory of gravity doesn't address the question of why there are no unicorns, so it must be wrong.

17. IGNORING THE ADVICE OF EXPERTS WITHOUT A GOOD REASON

Example: Sure, the experts think you shouldn't ride a bicycle into the eye of a hurricane, but I have my own theory.

18. FOLLOWING THE ADVICE OF KNOWN IDIOTS

Example: Uncle Billy says pork makes you smarter. That's good enough for me!

19. REACHING BIZARRE CONCLUSIONS WITHOUT ANY INFORMATION

Example: The car won't start. I'm certain the spark plugs have been stolen by rogue clowns.

20. FAULTY PATTERN RECOGNITION

Example: His last six wives were murdered mysteriously. I hope to be wife number seven.

21. FAILURE TO RECOGNIZE WHAT'S IMPORTANT

Example: My house is on fire! Quick, call the post office and tell them to hold my mail!

22. UNCLEAR ON THE CONCEPT OF SUNK COSTS

Example: We've spent millions developing a water-powered pogo stick. We can't stop investing now or it will all be wasted.

23. OVERAPPLICATION OF OCCAM'S RAZOR (WHICH SAYS THE SIMPLEST EXPLANATION IS USUALLY RIGHT)

Example: The simplest explanation for the moon landings is that they were hoaxes.

24. IGNORING ALL ANECDOTAL EVIDENCE

Example: I always get hives immediately after eating strawberries. But without a scientifically controlled experiment, it's not reliable data. So I continue to eat strawberries every day, since I can't tell if they cause hives.

25. INABILITY TO UNDERSTAND THAT SOME THINGS HAVE MULTIPLE CAUSES

Example: The Beatles were popular for one reason only: They were good singers.

26. JUDGING THE WHOLE BY ONE OF ITS CHARACTERISTICS

Example: The sun causes sunburns. Therefore, the planet would be better off without the sun.

27. BLINDING FLASHES OF THE OBVIOUS

Example: If everyone had more money, we could eliminate poverty.

28. BLAMING THE TOOL

Example: I bought an encyclopedia but I'm still stupid. This encyclopedia must be defective.

29. HALLUCINATIONS OF REALITY

Example: I got my facts from a talking tree.

30. TAKING THINGS TO THEIR ILLOGICAL CONCLUSION

Example: If you let your barber cut your hair, the next thing you know he'll be lopping off your limbs!

31. FAILURE TO UNDERSTAND WHY RULES DON'T HAVE EXCEPTIONS

Example: It should be legal to shoplift, as long as you don't take enough to hurt the company's earnings.

32. PROOF BY LACK OF EVIDENCE

Example: I've never seen you drunk, so you must be one of those Amish people.

8

Bringing Humor and Creativity to Your Job

I've heard it said that kindergartners already know how to sing and dance and paint. But as you've probably noticed, that only applies to your own kids. Everyone else's kids are just scribbling, shouting, and jumping around. Their interference is probably the only thing keeping your children's work out of the Louvre.

As far as I can tell, most people don't start life with much in the way of creative skills. And things go downhill from there. In fact, life is one huge process of eliminating any traces of creativity in order to make you more employable. By the time you enter the workforce, you've been scrubbed almost clean. Your employer takes it from there

There are undeniable economic reasons for eliminating creativity in workers. As a consumer, I know I wouldn't want my doctor to get too creative with me. I want him to give me the same thing that cured the last guy. The last thing you want to hear your doctor say is, "Hey, I wonder if one of these would fit in there!"

When I get on an airplane, I don't want a pilot with any creative urges either.

Air Traffic
Controller: Flight 399, take runway three.

Creative Pilot: I always take runway three. I thought I'd try landing on the roof of the terminal this time.

Air Traffic Controller: Pull up! Pull up!

Same thing with the police. I don't want to get stopped for speeding and be faced with any creativity options there either.

Cop: The rules say I'm supposed to give you a ticket for this sort of thing. But I like to be more creative.

Me: Um . . . what's that mean?

Cop: Greek wrestling.

Too much creativity in the wrong places is clearly bad. The problem with the societywide creativity-squashing system is that is has unintended consequences. Any system that eliminates dangerous creativity will eliminate good creativity too. And where there is no creativity, there is no room for happiness. My goal for the next section of this book is to teach you my special technique for becoming funnier and more creative at work. Most of it will actually be useful.

I treat humor and creativity as one topic because you need creativity to do humor. It comes in handy for other things too, obviously, but I'll focus on humor here.

▶ WHERE CREATIVITY COMES FROM

I can only speak for myself, but I believe my own creativity is 80 percent clever technique, 10 percent genetic abnormality (the good kind), and 10 percent exposure to secondhand smoke.

If you didn't get any secondhand smoke during your childhood development, it's never too late. If you want to make up for lost time, I recommend becoming a barfly or traveling to Europe.

If you're not an adult, and your parents won't let you go to bars or to Europe, you'll need to hang around with the bad kids to get your secondhand smoke. If you don't know any bad kids, I rent myself out as an invisible friend to kids who aren't popular enough to get one without paying. But that's a separate line of business, so send me an e-mail message if you'd like me to be your invisible friend.

For this book, I'll concentrate on the 80 percent of the creative process that is clever technique. That's where I can help the most. In the following section I'll teach you how to make time for creativity. Later, under the topic of humor, I'll get more specific about the techniques for improving creativity.

▶ MANAGE CREATIVITY, NOT TIME

Creativity comes in many forms. You could be creating a better business idea, a better software concept, a better process, or a better anything. Most adults feel they don't have time to develop their creative skills. My theory is that people don't actually have a shortage of time, they're just approaching the question in the wrong way.

Take this quiz to determine whether you understand the implications of good time management:

Time Management Quiz

If you are the first person on your team to finish your work, you will be rewarded with:

a. A huge bonus
b. Recognition as a rising star
c. More work

The surest way to be permanently unhappy is to manage your time.

"Managing time" is a concept that made perfect sense for jobs in the past, such as the job of picking bugs out of another monkey's fur.* The more time you dedicated to the task, the more bugs you got. It was simple math, even for monkeys. And the creative alternative—high-pressure steam cleaning—was deemed impractical due to the lack of electricity in the monkey kingdom. For

---

*In the interest of political correctness, since some Creationists will read this book and be offended by the indirect reference to evolution, you can substitute the word *apostle* for *monkey* and the point still holds.

monkeys, the time you spent on the job was clearly more important than the level of creativity you demonstrated. But enough about monkeys—I sometimes get carried away because they're so darned cute.

If you have a white-collar job, your best strategy is to manage your creativity, not your time. People who manage their creativity get happy and rich. People who manage their time get tired.

Ask yourself which headline you are more likely to see:

a.   CUBICLE WORKER BECOMES BILLIONAIRE THANKS TO CAREFUL SCHEDULING

or . . .

b.   POPE DECLARES VIOLENCE IS OKAY WITH HIM, AS LONG AS YOU HAVE A GOOD REASON

An effective way to select a career strategy is to compare it to the odds of the pope endorsing violence. If your strategy has similar odds, consider a new plan.

Scheduling is a blunt instrument when it comes to managing your life. An idea that changes the world can happen in an instant, at any time it pleases. Creativity doesn't need much time. Consider this inspirational little story:

A Little Story About Creativity

Somewhere in a vast wasteland of cubicles, copiers, and conference rooms, an idea is about to be born. It is just the soul of an idea, twinkling in and out of existence, waiting for the right combination of matter and energy to provide form and motion. While it waits, it watches, hidden just beyond the peripheral vision of the human inhabitants, teasing their collective imagination, then backing away, like a name you can't remember or the scent of something familiar. It has no weight or resistance. It is not part of reality. Yet somehow it interacts with reality. It is the mysterious force that appears according to some unpredictable schedule. This is its time. The probability field begins to collapse. Matter and energy are aligning in exactly the right configuration. The idea senses the invitation and begins an instant transformation from nothingness to somethingness. It sparks to life, tiny and weak, hovering just above the carpet. In time, with the right combination of hope and dreams and risk, the idea can become large enough to change the world.

Suddenly, the guy who delivers the copier paper comes around the corner and crushes the idea with his dolly. This is a bigger tragedy than anyone will ever know, because he's delivering the three-hole paper that your inconsiderate co-workers will leave in the copier to ambush you.

As you can see from this inspirational story, creativity doesn't require much time. But creativity always needs your energy. You can't create if you're pooped or your brain is full of junk. A person who manages creativity makes sure his schedule has lots of free spaces, no matter how many priorities are looming. You need a certain amount of free time to recharge your creative energy.

The obvious problem with my advice is that if you manage your life for maximum creativity, you end up looking like a lazy pig. You might as well put an apple in your mouth, spread some hay on the floor of your cubicle, and start napping with your arms and legs out to the side. But you can avoid unkind comparisons to any member of the animal kingdom by using the simple advice that follows. I'll teach you how to cleverly manage your creativity while appearing to be an imbecile who only manages his time.

While it's true that a complete focus on time management will ruin you, you still need *some* discipline in that area. You can't totally separate time management from creativity management. The point is, when you have to pick between managing your creativity and managing your time—and you often have to make that choice—favor creativity. That's where the payoff is.

Here's a true story about how the Human Resources department at one company uses technology to help keep the workload manageable:

From: [name withheld]
To: scottadams@aol.com

I have always thought that HR was staffed by idiots, but now I'm not so sure. After our last semiannual Reorganization Festival, I inadvertently came across the name of my new HR representative (yes, well, it was on the next-to-the-top document in my boss's in-basket, so it was almost in plain sight). I decided to call her just so she'd know that I knew who she was. I called the company operator to get her number.

Me: I'd like the number for Ima Ghost in HR, please.

Operator: I'm sorry, that number is unlisted.

Me:	I don't want her home number. I want her office number.
Operator:	Right. It's unlisted.
Me:	I'm an employee. She's my HR rep. I need to call her.
Operator:	I'm sorry.
Me:	I can't talk to my HR rep?
Operator:	Oh, you can talk to her if she calls you, but I can't give you her number. Sorry. (click)

Undaunted, I walked over to the last rumored location for HR. I found a locked office (at 10:00 A.M.) and a list of 800 numbers taped to the door.

I copied down the "If you need assistance" one and went back to the office. I called the number and tried the first option, which led to four more options, the first of which led to three more. I tried the first one again—it disconnected me. I called back and tried the 1–1–2 option—it disconnected me. Not easily dissuaded, I called every single option. They all disconnected me.

So, at my *Fortune* 50 company, we have HR reps with unlisted office phone numbers and an HR "Help" line that disconnects all callers with no human intervention. In fact, it would seem that there are no "humans" in "Human Resources." They're probably in an off-site conference at a local resort, laughing their asses off.

No matter what your job is, there are always more things to do than there are hours in the day. People who manage their time see a hole in their calendar and they fill it faster than a Clydesdale can fill a Dixie cup.

People who manage their creative energy will leave spaces in their day during their most creative hours. For most people, that's either late at night or early in the morning. If you work hard all day, you're probably too tired to use the late-night hours. By process of elimination, that leaves the early morning as the best time to be creative.

Do all your creative thinking in the morning. I recommend that you avoid scheduling any meetings or answering any phone calls before 9:00 A.M.

By the early-afternoon hours, if your brain is normal, it's running strictly on inertia and reflex. All you can do during those hours are the things that are exactly like other things you've done in similar situations. Creativity is out of the question. You might argue that you don't notice any difference in your thinking during the afternoon. That's because you're too dazed to notice anything during those hours. I'm sure that's true for me; I believe you could set my eyebrows on fire during the afternoon and I wouldn't notice until sometime the next morning.

I always schedule my noncreative activities during the afternoon. For example, today I have a meeting with two important business partners. There's no real agenda. The only purpose is to make a personal connection. I guess the reason we're doing it is so that later, if we talk by telephone, we can close our eyes and imagine what each other looks like. It's a poor man's version of videoconferencing.

Creativity Tip

When you imagine other people, to the extent that they are clothed, always put them in white culottes. That way you don't use up any extra memory space for their wardrobe. You can use the extra memory for storing creative things. Culottes work for any gender because they're half pants and half skirt. No need to chew up extra memory space for each gender. The only exception to the culottes rule is dressing the elderly. You don't want to see their spindly legs, so put them in blue sweatpants.

Today's meeting will be at 2:00 P.M., a time when my brain automatically shuts down all systems not directly related to organ functions. If you did a Turing* test on me, I would not pass. I suspect that my end of the conversation will not be described by anyone later as "scintillating." It'll probably go like this:

Me: Hi. Nice to see you.

Guests: Hi. Nice to see you.

Me: So, are you two married to each other?

Guests: Um, no, we work together.

Me: Too bad. You'd make a nice couple. Would you like a beverage?

It will go downhill from there.

---

*A Turing test is what you use to determine if a computer can display intelligence that is indistinguishable from human intelligence. No computer has passed the test yet. But that's only because no one has written a program to make a computer complain about its job all day.

MULTITASKING

You can create more time for yourself by combining mind-numbingly boring tasks (i.e., your job) with fascinating creative tasks (i.e., preparing for your cool new future job). Let's call this process "creative multitasking" so it sounds important.

Creative multitasking works magic because creativity and boredom go together like salt on french fries. No one ever says, "I don't need any french fries, I already have salt." The more you have of one, the easier it is to consume the other. Work can be like that too if you choose your challenges wisely. The more boredom you endure, the more ready your mind will be to take on something interesting. And the more creative stimulation you take on, the more appreciative you'll be of any opportunity to do something boring to give your brain a rest.

Never make the mistake of trying to multitask by combining a boring activity with another boring activity. Your brain will subconsciously associate that level of boredom with old age and send the signal to grow more hair in your ears. And don't multitask with two creative tasks either, such as knitting and ballet. That's just begging for trouble. If you're going to multitask, choose your tasks wisely.

If you work in a cubicle, you already have the boring part of the equation worked out. Look for creative activities that can blend in with the day job without arousing suspicion. For example, if you spend a lot of time on the phone, start a phone-sex business to release your creativity. Your phone-sex customers won't get suspicious if you toss in some corporate phrases such as "Leverage your team member!" and "Enhance the performance of your business unit!" Anyone listening at the office will just think you're bossy and foul-mouthed. That never hurt anyone's career. And if your boss happens to call you on the sex line, that can be a big advantage for your next performance review.

If you don't like talking about sex, try writing a novel in your cubicle. Do it one paragraph at a time, using your e-mail software. Send each installment to your home e-mail account for assembly later. If someone looks over your shoulder, apparently you're composing a brief e-mail message. If your computer hard drive gets audited, not a trace of personal business will be found. I have spoken to several people who are working on their first book in this fashion. (Really.)

Here's a story about someone who almost got away with multitasking two boring jobs, but ultimately it didn't work out. It's a valuable lesson to us all.

From: [name withheld]
To: scottadams@aol.com

This is a true story of a computer programmer who worked as an independent consultant at (company name) in New York City.

The consultant had an interview with a manager on the second floor of the (company) building. He accepted the job. A few days later a second agency he worked with sent him for an interview with another manager of the same company, on the fourth floor of the same building. He accepted that job as well.

He managed to work both of these full-time, 8:00 to 5:00 jobs for over six months without anyone realizing what was going on. He would arrive early for one job, about 7:45, before anyone else got there. Then about 10:00 he would walk down the stairs and show up for the second position, where they believed he was one of those programmers who like to work a later schedule.

He worked little more than eight hours a day but was able to bill for sixteen by convincing each department that he was working full-time just for it.

I know this is true because he was fired just a couple of weeks before I started there. A couple of employees were still shocked and told me the story over lunch. I later asked some other people about it, and they confirmed that it had actually happened.

In the end he was caught when someone from one floor went to the other and saw him working there.

Tip: If you ever get the opportunity to pretend you have two full-time jobs in the same building, cover your tracks by telling everyone how happy you are to be working in the same building as your identical twin.

LOOKING BUSY

The secret to carving out huge chunks of free time from your job is to make your cubicle or office look as though you'll be right back. Meanwhile you can be off creating interesting things, taking challenging classes, or just going on holiday. If you keep up with your e-mail and voice-mail, few people will be the wiser.

To give your cubicle that "back in a flash" look, use a combination of these tricks:

1. Leave a spare jacket on the hanger. No one goes home without his or her jacket.

2. Turn on your computer. (Make sure it's password-protected so you don't get stung by the pranks I explained earlier in the book.)

3. Open a computer software manual to a difficult topic.

4. If you wear glasses, but not all the time, leave your old pair on the technical manual as though you had just set them down. If you don't wear glasses, get some.

You'll need a quiet place to do your creative work while you're avoiding your day job. If you drive to work, you can sit in your car in the parking lot. It's like a home office with a stereo. If you have a cellular phone, you can check your voice mail from a safe distance and be ready to spring into action if an emergency arises.

For those of you who are willing to make a major investment in avoiding work, move to a home that's near your job. After you "stage" your cubicle in the morning, just drive home and enjoy a leisurely brunch. Head back to the office right before lunch. As everyone is leaving for lunch, complain that you will have to work straight through. That will give you all the "face time" you need. When everyone leaves for lunch, use the hour to surf the Web in your cubicle, free from the teamwork and assignments that would normally divert you.

From: [name withheld]
To: scottadams@aol.com

There's a method of "work simulation" that I use almost every day. It's not really funny but it is VERY effective.

I have a laptop as well as a desktop PC on my desk with the backs facing toward the door to my office. I keep my door open so nobody can say I'm trying to hide something, or avoid work. On my laptop, a Web browser is constantly running. On my desktop, my e-mail software is just as vigilant. When I hear someone coming my way, I start rolling my chair back and forth between the computers at a feverish pace, all the while keeping a disturbed look on my face. The intruder will then—without fail—ask if this is a bad time. I will stop between the computers and with my eyes quickly shifting between the two say, "Well . . . no. What's up?"

Usually, the person will assume it's a bad time and leave quickly. But sometimes a visitor is pushy and wants to come in and have a seat. When this happens, I will make eye contact and listen for a while, then slide over and hit a few keys on one of the computers, mumble something, then make eye contact again as if I hadn't moved. Most people become uneasy and leave.

From: [name withheld]
To: scottadams@aol.com

I wrote a program that displays a window on my screen
that reads "Compiling! Do Not Touch!" It also has a status
bar that moves across the window so it looks like it's actually doing something.

Whenever I sneak out or I'm just sleeping, I run that program. If anyone surprises me at my desk or looks at my
screen while I'm away, it looks like I'm a busy guy.

From: [name withheld]
To: scottadams@aol.com

The best way to look busy is to look angry.

From: [name withheld]
To: scottadams@aol.com

This trick always works. Grab a large stack of important-looking papers or an expensive piece of portable equipment and tools. Next, get a VERY contorted look on your face and briskly walk right past your boss muttering gibberish the entire time. Walk to the nearest meeting room, spread out the whole mess on a conference table, and close the door. Your boss will presume this is a very difficult problem. You may now enjoy several hours of peace and quiet.

How long can you keep your job while doing no work whatsoever? I know several people who are apparently conducting long-term trials to determine the answer to that question. The tricky part is explaining what you've been doing all year when it becomes clear that your projects all failed because of your laziness. But if you're lucky enough to be involved with projects that fail for reasons unrelated to your lack of involvement, your trail of sloth can be covered indefinitely.

AVOIDING WORK BY BEING TOO BUSY

If you're too ethical to use cheap tricks to avoid work, you can accomplish the same thing by being so busy that people learn to avoid you. I don't recommend this approach unless you're already in what I call Stage Three of being overworked.

FOUR STAGES OF BEING OVERWORKED

Stage One: Your entire day is filled with one crisis after another.

Stage Two: Your entire day is spent explaining to people that your entire day is filled with one crisis after another.

Stage Three: Your entire day is spent apologizing for the crises you didn't handle because you spent your entire day explaining to other people that your day was filled with crises.

Stage Four: You're so busy that no one even dares call you.

Many people make the mistake of trying to lighten their workload to make time for creative projects. That strategy can never work. If you're an adult, there is no stage below Stage One. If your co-workers, family, friends, and business partners find out that your schedule is not filled with life-threatening crises, they will happily supply them.

It's impossible to free your schedule if other people find out you're doing less work. Your co-workers will try to divert your newly created free time to solving their problems. It's called team-work, and you should avoid it at all costs.

You will never be able to make time for your creative projects by trying to become less busy. Your only path to freedom is to INCREASE your workload until you reach Stage Four. You have to make yourself so busy with important work that no reasonable person would expect you to do anything more. That's when you can stop doing any work whatsoever. Everyone will assume you are so busy helping other people—because that's the kind of per-son you are—that it would be rude and insensitive to ask you to do more. This is the technique used by CEOs, and it explains why they can take six weeks of vacation every year without hurting the company, but you can't.

BEING UNHELPFUL

In the course of your business day, many people will come to you for assistance. If you make the mistake of being helpful, those people will be back tomorrow. They might even spread the word of your helpfulness. Soon, complete strangers will be trying to get free help from you. The best way to avoid these parasites—a.k.a. co-workers—is to be astonishingly unhelpful, as in these examples.

I'll Meet You There: If one of your co-workers is incessantly bugging you to help on his project, agree to have a meeting with him in a faraway conference room at an agreed time. You buy yourself some free time up front by quickly agreeing to the meeting. And you also get at least thirty minutes while your co-worker sits waiting for you, gently cursing your name for never showing up. Eventually he will hunt you down or call you. Act surprised that it's so late and say you just need to make one more call. Having been on the receiving end of this technique many times, I can assure you that it not only works, but it works repeatedly with the same victims.

Smoking Breaks: If you don't already smoke, consider starting. In the long run you'll die a horrible death, but in the short run you'll get the benefits of being a social pariah who takes too many smoking breaks throughout the day. Nonsmokers have learned the futility of reasoning with smokers, so you'll be able to interrupt any business activity to take your smoking breaks. If you want to end an unproductive meeting with a nonsmoker, invite him to join you on your smoking break so you can talk. Most nonsmokers will discover they have something else they need to do instead.

Harnessing the Power of Your Own Incompetence: If you're naturally incompetent, you already know the freedom and joy that come from being that way. Your co-workers learn to avoid giving you any work that matters, thus freeing your mind to do more of whatever the hell it is that people like you do. If you're not incompetent, you might want to take some tips from this star performer.

From: [name withheld]
To: scottadams@aol.com

A colleague and I wrote a paper for a conference that we were scheduled to attend the following week. On Monday we asked the group secretary to copy it onto the department letterhead, telling her we needed it by Thursday. "No problem," she said. Later that afternoon we realized that a minor change needed to be made and I asked the secretary for the report back. She squirmed in her chair and asked if she could get it to me tomorrow. Next morning, same thing, "Try back after lunch." Early afternoon came and she said, "Not today, maybe tomorrow."

"What," I asked, "happened to our report?"

"Oh," she said, "I had so many things on my desk to do yesterday that I put them all in an interdepartmental mail envelope and mailed them to myself. Then my desk is clear and I look like I'm getting all my work done. I will work on the report when it comes back in a day or two."

Wednesday afternoon the envelope returned. I snagged the report and never asked her to do another thing again.

NEW ETIQUETTE FOR EFFICIENCY

Two hundred years ago, when there weren't many people on earth, everyone was perfectly happy to listen to stories about anything from tree bark to bunions. This was before electricity was popular, so a good bunion story was better than sitting in the dark doing nothing.

But now we have television to fill the voids in our lives. Still, we often get trapped listening to people who have nothing interesting to say. This can chew up vast blocks of your precious time.

I think we should all agree to revise the standard rules of etiquette to allow a polite way to escape that sort of person. Maybe something like this:

Etiquette Decree:

All people must carry a card that lists their boring stories, including the running time for each. It is the right of any citizen to examine another person's story card in advance and decide whether the story is worth the time.

Bob's Story Card

The Car That Just Wouldn't Start:	Running time 14 minutes
Rake Hit Me in the Groin:	Running time 18 minutes
Damn Dog Ate My Biscuit:	Running time 12 minutes
Why I Hate Art:	Running time 83 minutes

After examining the story card, the potential story victim would have an opportunity to politely decline the abuse, using this suggested form:

> I'd rather not waste ____ minutes of my mortality listening to a story about your toddler's appetite for crayons. But if there's a change my limited time situation, such as the surprising discovery that I am immortal, I will contact you immediately.

This might seem unkind, but it wouldn't be rude if we all agree on the rules. And it makes sense; even a can of peas has a label that shows what's in it. All I ask is that boring people be held to the same safety standard as all the other vegetables.

Here's a story card that you can fill out for a boring co-worker of yours, after you've heard all of his stories several times:

_____'s Boring Story List
Name

BORING STORY TOPIC   RUNNING TIME

_____   _____

_____   _____

_____   _____

_____   _____

_____   _____

_____   _____

_____   _____

_____   _____

HOW TO SAY NO

In a typical day, the majority of your creative energy will be hijacked by the people around you, primarily your co-workers. For example, just today I was hit up for these unreasonable favors, which I quote:

▶ "May I get a word in edgewise?"

▶ "Please back your car off my foot!"

▶ "Would you mind not staring at my chest for two
    seconds?"

Imagine how unproductive my day would be if I did what
everyone else wanted me to do instead of focusing on my own priorities. Luckily, I have developed a system for saying no to people
who try to steer me off the path of creative success. I share these
secrets with you, in the hope that I never have to borrow anything
from you.

Sounding Pathetic: I have the sort of telephone voice that makes

people ask if I'm sick. With me it's natural, but you can fake it if
you try. If I get twenty calls in a day, fourteen will ask me if science has a cure for whatever I have. It used to be annoying, but
I realized it worked to my advantage. It makes me sound overworked and pathetic. Sympathy is a powerful tool if you want to
weasel out of favors. If you play it right, you can convince the
person on the other end of the phone that you're too weak to
survive any requests for assistance. But always act as though

you're willing to risk it. You don't have to lie. Just let your raspy voice send the misleading signal on its own.

For example, let's say your friend calls and asked this favor:

Friend: Would you help me move some furniture?

You: (raspy and pathetic voice) Is it heavy?

Friend: Well, yeah, that's the point.

You: I could move some knickknacks maybe. Not the big ones. Is that the sort of thing you had in mind?

Friend: Um . . .

You: When I say I could move knickknacks, I don't mean I could lift and carry them. But I could push them to new locations on the shelf.

Friend: Never mind.

You: How about doilies? Do you have any of those in the wrong place? I'm eager to help.

At this point in the conversation, even the densest person will conclude that you must be very sick. He will want to hang up quickly, because you have captured the favor-asking high ground. He knows that at any moment you might ask him to bring you some soup.

Acting Confused: Ideally you want the person you are rejecting to feel foolish for imposing on you. You can do that by asking questions as if you do not understand the request. For example, let's say someone asks you to drive him to the airport during the workday so he can begin his vacation. The wrong approach would be to say exactly what you're thinking:

WRONG

> "You selfish turdling! Since when did I become the source of financing for your vacations? Have you heard of a new invention called the taxi? You make me want to puke."

You can see how the honest response would cause trouble in your relationship later. The correct approach is to act confused and continue to ask for clarification:

CORRECT

Friend:	Would you take me to the airport tomorrow?
You:	Are you asking me to quit my job and travel the world with you?
Friend:	Um, no, I just want a ride to the airport.
You:	Did someone steal your car?
Friend:	No.
You:	Taxi strike?
Friend:	No.
You:	Well, now I'm really confused.
Friend:	Look, I'll owe you a favor.
You:	Can I have my favor in advance?
Friend:	I guess that's fair. What do you want?
You:	I want you to take a cab to the airport.

Saying Yes but Never Doing It: The most time-efficient w~~ay~~ no to something is to say yes, and then never do it. If your o~~bjec~~tive is to save yourself time and effort, it's counterproductive to say no to someone, even if you have a bulletproof reason. No matter how good the reason, you will be interrogated further, under the inquisitor's assumption that you are either a lazy, stinkin' liar or you are a lazy, stinkin' idiot who can't think of a way to fit something new into your schedule. This can be both insulting and very accurate. That's why it hurts so much.

To avoid that type of pain, cheerily say yes and then get on with your life as though you had said no. You will build goodwill instead of suffering insult and interrogation. It might seem as though you will pay for your spineless deception later, but observation shows that is rarely the case. My brother discovered this technique as a teen. When Mom would ask him to take out the garbage, he always responded with a cheery "Okay." Then he continued reading his comic books. The pattern would repeat for hours. Mom would get increasingly annoyed with each new request. In response, my brother would become increasingly cheery and agreeable.

"Right away, Mom! I'm on it."

But the garbage never moved. Eventually Mom would recognize the pattern and do the only thing you can do when you have an unresponsive teenager: Reassign the work to the preteen. I've toted a lot of garbage in my day. My brother is a genius.

I've since modified the say-yes technique so it doesn't sound quite so unhelpful. Now I quickly agree to do whatever I'm asked by saying, "Sure! Glad to help. I have about six hundred other favors to do first, but yours is definitely on my list. If there's anything else I can do, don't hesitate to ask."

This serves to lower people's expectations to the point where they will immediately seek alternatives for whatever they needed. With this method you can usually get people to call you before their deadline to tell you it's "already taken care of." They might even thank you for your help. Be gracious and offer to be of assistance in the future. Never say, "How's it feel to suck your own blood, you parasite?" That just causes ill will.

Here's a true report from the field that shows how useful this technique can be.

From: [name withheld]
To: scottadams@aol.com

Last summer I was working on a number of Web pages, and once they were finished, they were placed on the company server so that my co-workers could look at them and give me feedback on them. Fortunately, most of my co-workers are at least semi-Internet-literate, but one was not. This co-worker surfed outside my pages to a new government site and found errors on it. She called me to inform me of these errors. I explained that the government Website was totally out of my control, but she insisted I write the Web master to tell him of the errors. Her rationale was that if we linked to pages that had a few problems, my company would look bad. Knowing that I would just confuse her if I tried to explain the concept of the Internet to her, I just agreed politely and ignored it. Problem solved.

Preemptive Voice-mail Declines: Lately I've been experimenting with using voice-mail to do preemptive turn-downs. My outgoing voice-mail message anticipates most of the typical requests for my time and delivers the bad news without my direct involvement. It changes frequently, but here's a template for your use:

> Hi, this is Scott Adams. At the sound of the beep, please leave your long, rambling message explaining why I should do something that benefits you— something with little or no value to the rest of the solar system. I will send my answer to you via a coded message in your television set. If the answer is no, Larry King will be wearing suspenders tonight. If the answer is yes, *Good Morning America* will announce that their new morning host is Salman Rushdie.

Most people will persist even after hearing the message. But I've found that it softens them up considerably and they don't fight too hard when I say no in person.

Referring People to Your Web Page: If people are always asking you for information, start referring them to your Web page. It's okay if you don't have a Web page, or that your Web page has no useful information. Most people are delighted when you tell them all the information is on your Web page. I guess that sounds like a very cool thing, so they appreciate it at some level. Then they go away.

Saying No in Writing: The best way to say no to something is in writing. That gives you the freedom to completely misinterpret the request, so you can decline using any excuse whatsoever. For example, if someone leaves you a voice mail asking for your help choosing a software vendor, reply by e-mail and say that you can't help because you "already donate to the United Way." Obviously your answer has nothing to do with the question, but it will look like a simple misunderstanding.

SECRETARIES

Never get yourself a secretary. People who have secretaries usually end up with more work than the people who have none.

Every unit of efficiency provided by a secretary will be balanced by a counterefficiency.

Efficiency	Counterefficiency
Takes phone messages.	Writes fours that look like nines, twos that look like sevens, and sevens that look like ones.
Intercepts hundreds of unproductive requests.	Creates thousands of unproductive requests for your time.
Schedules meetings for you.	Schedules meetings with people you'd rather see on milk cartons.
Organizes the diversity workshop for the department.	Accuses you of discrimination.
Keeps time-wasting people out of your office.	Won't stay out of your office.
Buys a gift for your spouse for Valentine's Day.	Expects a gift for birthdays, Secretary's Day, and whatever else Hallmark decides.
Reduces your stress by handling tasks that you would find frustrating.	Increases your stress by sharing personal problems you've never even heard of before.
Files important documents . . .	. . . where you can't find them.

Dogbert Disconnect

I've noticed that about 20 percent of my business calls result in me being put on hold and forgotten or simply disconnected immediately. Being a trusting soul, normally I might assume that multiline telephones are inherently confusing and that busy people make mistakes. But I once worked in a job that involved helping people over the phone, so I know the ugly truth.

In one of my first jobs, at a large bank, I was being trained to work in a customer service department. My trainer excused himself to answer a ringing phone. He put the customer on hold and resumed my training. The lesson for that day was how to make a phone call go away by putting a customer on hold and ignoring him. It worked! I asked my trainer if he ever got in trouble for doing that. He assured me that it's a problem only if you give your real name—always a big mistake in the banking industry. To this day, most of my co-workers think they worked with a short, blond guy named Pat McGroin.

People who work in technical support jobs deal with huge numbers of morons each day. Naturally they have developed the most sophisticated methods for avoiding callers. For example, if you call a tech support number within thirty minutes of the end of their work shift, you will automatically be put on hold for thirty minutes, then disconnected. No tech support person wants to take a chance on getting the call from hell right before closing time. They're professional problem solvers; it's no wonder they figured out how to solve their own problems.

CHANGE YOUR NAME

If you've got a name that's long, or hard to spell, change it to something more efficient. It will save you months over the course of your life. That's time you can use for having fun. My name, for example, is mercifully efficient: Scott Adams. It's easy to spell and it's economical with letters. I can fill out forms like a demon. When someone asks my name, I say it once and I'm off to do other things. The savings add up. I wrote this entire book in the amount of time that Boutros Boutros-Ghali spends trying to rent a car.

Throughout history, the most productive and successful people have been the ones with easy names.

SUCCESSFUL NAMES

Cher

Madonna

Mister T

President John Adams

President John Q. Adams

Only rarely do people with complicated names become successful. They are "the exceptions that prove the rule." Arnold Schwarzenegger is a perfect example. When he was a teenager, the forearm on his writing hand became huge from writing his name on school assignments. The other kids called him "Big Arm." He was forced to lift weights with the other arm so the one oversized arm didn't make him walk in circles. The rest is history.

Consider The Artist Formerly Known As Prince. When he was just called Prince, he had a hit movie and some top-ten albums. When his name was efficient, his career boomed. But then he tried to change his name to that strange symbol thing. He's spent every day since then just trying to make a withdrawal from his bank. I don't know if he still plays an instrument or not.

AVOIDING WORK BY ACTING CREATIVE

An effective way to reduce your workload is to act creative, which is exactly like acting insane but without the involuntary incarceration and ensuing social stigma. It's somewhat similar to being a Technology Prima Donna, but without the burden of pretending to have technical skill.

ACTING CREATIVE

Boss: Does anyone have a status on the project?

You: THE HAIR IN MY NOSE IS PLOTTING TO KILL US!!!

Boss: Remind me not to invite him to the next meeting.

At the next meeting, while the uncreative people are worrying that their fat cells are establishing trading colonies in their buttocks, you'll be off alone, having a good time.

If you want to be known as a creative person, it's important to stay in character all day long. When someone asks you a question, don't be quick to answer. Instead, stare at nothing for an uncomfortably long period and scrunch your eyebrows with a faint suggestion that a Trident-class submarine is navigating through your intestines. Make obscure references to dead people or old movies and act as if everyone should know exactly what you're talking about. This will kill the conversation deader than a shrunken head at a Hacky Sack festival.

Now look at the ground and say something ambiguous that could be construed as either an insult, or a threat, or possibly just a poorly delivered joke. If you're consistent, this type of behavior will buy you some time to be alone so you can create things.

Whatever you do, don't let anyone know that you have math skills, if in fact you have any. Math skill is a sure sign that you're an impostor trying to pass as a creative person. Go out of your way to act math-stupid. For example, after dinner at a restaurant with friends, say, "Okay, there are four of us, we all had the same thing, and the check comes to $40. Did anyone bring a calculator?"

As a creative person, you are not obliged to be logical, since logic is the opposite of creativity. Act confused at every opportunity. If you get into a discussion of world events, take an irrational stand and defend it vigorously. Here are some good positions to take on important issues:

OPINIONS FOR CREATIVE PEOPLE

▶ Animals should be allowed to drive if they can pass the written test.

▶ Maybe we can't reduce global warming by opening our refrigerators at the same time, but shouldn't we at least try?

▶ The smart businesses always lose money, for tax reasons. Why can't we be like that?

FILTERING BAD IDEAS

Are you a good listener? By that I mean when someone talks to you, do you make eye contact and nod your head while thinking about yourself?

You don't have to listen to every single word that people say in order to be a good listener. You can usually get the gist of the topic in the first sentence, then tune out and nod politely until the noise stops. This method is sufficient to get 100 percent of the useful content from most conversations. For example, if someone says, "I'm sad that my goldfish died," and then the person continues talking about the fish, you can safely summarize the entire ensuing conversation—no matter its duration—into "I'm sad that my goldfish died." There's almost nothing that can be added to the goldfish story that will change the basic facts:

1. Fish dead
2. Owner sad

The rest of the story will involve details that are important to the owner of the deceased fish but not to you. You really don't need to know the precise time of day the fish died or the presumed cause of death. Nor do you need to know the ex-fish's name. It's dead. It will not come when called. If you feed it, it will not eat. Soon it will smell bad. It will more likely be flushed down the toilet than buried at Arlington. You can know many things without paying attention.

If you listen to other people at all, you will be forced to hear many incredibly bad suggestions and ideas during the course of your lifetime. You'll need some techniques to filter the 1 percent good ideas from the 99 percent bad ones. This can be a huge time-saver.

No one is smart enough to know in advance what ideas will turn out to be in the 1 percent, but sometimes you can filter out the most worthless ones, thus improving your odds of finding the winners. Over the years I have developed these handy rules for filtering out the worst ideas. These rules actually work:

RULES FOR FILTERING OUT BAD IDEAS

1. An opinion based on someone's **physical** reaction is better than an opinion based on someone's **thinking**.

2. An **unsolicited** opinion is more useful than one you ask for.

3. It doesn't matter how many people **dislike** an idea. All that matters is how many **like** it.

4. A sensible idea with small **upside potential** is a bad idea.

You'll be amazed at how useful the four rules are for weeding out bad ideas. See for yourself by trying them in this exercise.

EXERCISE—FIND THE BAD IDEAS

Determine if any of the following ideas are bad. Apply the four filtering rules to each one. If the idea fails any one of the four filters, it is a bad idea.

IDEAS:

A. "Since you asked, yes, your meat loaf is delicious and you should certainly open a chain of stores to sell it."

B. "It's none of my business, and I'm a complete stranger, but I think you should do something about that mole on your forehead. You look like a damn unicorn."

C. "Personally, I don't like the idea of an antigravity invention, so you probably ought to spend your time doing something more useful."

D. "*Dilbert* books arouse me. Someone should write more of them."

E. "You should try rock climbing!"

The filters are deceptively simple, but amazingly effective. If you use them, it will save you vast amounts of time weeding out the bad ideas, without missing any good ideas in the process.

► CREATING HUMOR

In this section, I will teach you my *Dilbert*-honed secret formula for turning annoying and frustrating workplace situations into healthy doses of mirth. Once you learn the secret techniques, you'll no longer look upon your co-workers as troublemaking dolts. They will become the raw materials feeding your humor engine. Your boss will seem to transform from an uncaring troll to a gold mine of laugh potential. Once you know the humor secrets, your workplace will suddenly seem like a very amusing place to spend the day.

Some employees use all their energy maneuvering for political advantage. That's called being Machiavellian. After you learn the humor secrets, you can spend your day mocking those employees. I call that Mockiavellian. Given a choice, you will always be happier as a Mockiavellian than a Machiavellian. And since you will seem funnier (and therefore smarter), those Machiavellian employees will eventually work for you. Then you can mock them even more.

ORIGINALITY

For humor to work, it must be original. It's easy to create original humor—or anything else original—if you follow my formula.

Originality Formula

Theft + Lack of talent + Time = Originality

Identify someone who has more creative talent than you do, then try to imitate that person exactly. If you're like me, you can depend on your lack of talent to make your imitation look nothing like the source. Over time, you'll drift even further from the source of your theft, thus becoming "original."

Just a coincidence?

Peanuts © UFS, Inc.   Dilbert © UFS, Inc.

The only way your imitation will be detected is if it looks too similar to the source. If you're cursed with enough talent to be a good imitator, try mixing stolen elements from different sources together until the result is unrecognizable.

In many ways, originality is like car theft. You should have the decency to change the license plates and repaint the car before you drive it past the original owner. That's just common courtesy.

My advice might sound cynical, but as far as I can tell, theft is the only way anyone approaches originality, with the exception of the clinically insane. The difference between what looks original and what looks derivative is the degree to which the theft has been disguised.

PICKING THE COMEDY TOPIC

The hardest part of writing humor is finding a topic that hasn't already been used more times than the only back scratcher at the

Institute of Very Itchy People. Ideally, you want a situation that makes you smile even before the humor has been added. If you start with a fresh and inherently funny situation, you're halfway home. Here are some topics from the corporate world that make you laugh before the joke is added:

NATURALLY FUNNY WORK TOPICS

▶ Teamwork

▶ Employee of the Week

▶ Cubicles

▶ ISO 9000

If a topic makes you gag, or clench your buns, or laugh, or sigh, or retch—or react physically in any way—you have a winner. The best situations are the ones that cause your body to react. Otherwise, it's just information without any emotional charge.

Emotion is the essence of humor. That's why it's impossible to do a joke about an object—like a cubicle—unless you add the human element. What's funny about cubicles is how they make people feel. Cubicles can inspire a wide range of emotions:

CUBICLE-RELATED EMOTIONS

▶ Despair that you haven't earned an office

▶ Comfort of being in your own little womb

▶ Jealousy at the people who have doors

▶ Anger at all the noise from neighboring cubicles

▶ Paranoia that passersby notice you're not working

▶ Claustrophobia

▶ Pride in your own little patch of real estate

▶ Feeling trapped by obnoxious co-workers

The most common dead end in trying to write jokes is to focus on objects instead of emotions. For example, one of the most frequently suggested topics for *Dilbert* is "bunk cubicles." The idea is that employees would be stacked in cubicles, like bunk beds. The idea is so visually appealing that it would be easy to construct a gag around the physical appearance of a bunk cubicle. But that would be a dead end. A bunk cubicle, however clever, is still just an object. It wouldn't come alive unless the focus of the joke was on how the employees felt about the idea of being treated like stackable objects. If I were to use the bunk cubicle idea, I would probably avoid drawing a picture of it at all, instead focusing on how the employees react to the concept.

Once you have your topic, you're ready to apply the "Two of Six" rule.

THE "TWO OF SIX" RULE

Some humor experts say the secret to humor is to combine something unexpected with something bad and then make sure it's happening to someone else. But if that's all it took, serial killers would be winning comedy competitions. The evening news is full of unexpected bad things that happen to other people. Most of it isn't funny, unless it involves exploding whales, ear biting, or pies thrown at billionaires.

Plenty of jokes don't have pain. If all jokes had to have pain, some of the most famous jokes in the world would have to be rewritten like this:

Q: Why did the chicken cross the road?
A: Because it was on fire.

Q: Why does a fireman wear red suspenders?
A: Maybe he's on fire too.

While it might be true that most humor has surprise, pain, and distance, that's not very useful information. It won't help you be funny. And there are too many exceptions. Something is clearly missing. That's why I developed a more useful framework for creating humor. I call it the "Two of Six Rule." It's based on my observation that all humor uses at least two of these six dimensions:

SIX DIMENSIONS OF HUMOR

1. Cuteness
2. Meanness
3. Bizarreness
4. Recognizability
5. Naughtiness
6. Cleverness

It doesn't matter which two dimensions you use. It doesn't matter if you use more than two. The only rule is that you have to use at least two of the six.

The way you use this framework is to select a topic that lends itself to one of the dimensions, for example, something that's inherently cute. Then you brainstorm with the other five dimensions to see which one can be layered on to your topic without causing confusion.

The framework alone isn't enough to guarantee laughs. It's

just a starting point. I'll give you some additional tips that can get you 80 percent of the way to Laughville. I'll expand on each of the six dimensions so you can see some examples and get a better idea how to apply them.

CUTENESS

By cuteness, I mean the quality that kids and animals have naturally. Anything with fur is cute, at least until you hit it with your car or make a coat out of it.

Things with big eyes and tiny noses are generally cute, with the possible exception of Michael Jackson. And the jury is still out on the animated cast of *South Park*.

You know cuteness when you see it. There's no strict definition. One thing is for sure: Dogs with hats are always cute.

Do not include in the cute category the adults who believe that although they are not good-looking in the classic sense, they are nonetheless cute.

I used to think I was in that category, but no one supported my claim. So now I tell people I'm inexplicably sexy instead. This position is more defensible because sexiness is more subjective than cute. For example, when you watch a nature program on television and see two love-crazed wolverines going at it like a couple of love-crazed wolverines, you don't say to yourself, "I gotta get me some of that."

No, you don't. But I sure do. Wolverines turn me on. That's my point: Everyone has a different idea of what is sexy.

Now, watch me seamlessly tie this back to the topic.

Unlike sex appeal, where everyone has his own opinion, people generally agree about what is cute. If you have a situation that involves kids or animals, you're halfway home, unless they're ugly kids. All you need to turn a cute situation into a funny situation is another dimension. Meanness is always a good dimension to mix with cuteness. For example, Barney the dinosaur is cute. But Barney the shish kebab is funny. It's cute, it's mean, it's all you need.

Meanness isn't the only thing you can add to cute. It's just the simplest. Here's an example of cuteness and meanness with a dash of cleverness in the form of a play on words.

The following example combines cuteness with meanness and adds a very indirect layer of "I've been there" recognizability.

MEANNESS

When you add meanness to a situation, the humor can easily degenerate into something sophomoric. For example, if you took a Tickle Me Elmo doll, which is cute, and then did something mean with it—like using it to light the charcoal grill at the kindergarten picnic—it would be funny, but somewhat juvenile. I do not condone that sort of humor.

I recommend a more mature approach to cruelty. The meanness should be subtler and more complicated. But it can still involve a Tickle Me Elmo doll. For example, consider this story about a thrifty family.

The parents are too cheap to buy their young daughter the thing she wants more than anything else in the world: a Tickle Me Elmo doll. Instead, the parents decide to rent an Elmo for one month, in the hope their daughter will lose interest before it is time to return it. The daughter, Tina, is delighted with the Elmo and plays with it for thirty straight days, loving it more every day.

At the end of the month, while Tina is at school, the parents return Elmo to the rental store. Wishing to avoid an ugly situation when Tina comes home, they invent a little white lie to explain Elmo's disappearance. They decide to tell Tina that Elmo died because she didn't feed him.

To support their story, the parents decide to bury something in the backyard. The logical choice is the neighbor's Great Dane, because the dog comes when called, thus eliminating the need to lug something heavy. The neighbors hear their dog barking and come outside to see what all the noise is about. Thinking fast, Tina's parents whack the neighbors with shovels and bury them instead of the dog. The neighbors' relatives, all of whom were on the way over for a family reunion, hear the screams and run to the rescue. Tina's parents—by this time quite handy with shovels—slay all of the neighbors' relatives and add them to the pile. Someone calls the police. The sound of shovel whacking fills the air. Eventually the pile in the backyard gets so large that the family opens a luxury ski resort and becomes multimillionaires.

The moral of the story: If life gives you lemons, build a luxury ski resort.

As you can see from that story, there's no law that says your humor can't be mixed with an inspirational message. But watch out when you mix cuteness with meanness. Not everyone is mature enough to realize how funny that sort of thing is.

If you don't feel comfortable taking your meanness all the way to genocide, you can still get plenty of traction by concentrating on rudeness. Rudeness is mean, and almost no one is offended by hearing a story about someone else's rudeness.

BIZARRENESS

Bizarreness refers to any two things that don't belong together. A rhinoceros on a bicycle is bizarre. Managers who care about your personal life are bizarre. Employees who complain of being overpaid are bizarre.

In comics, the most popular way to achieve bizarreness is with animals who act like people. You're halfway home if you have a talking animal, especially if the animal is cute. That's why you see so many cute, talking animals in comics.

Dogbert can say things that only sound funny because he's a little white dog. This cartoon is a perfect example of dialogue that is funny only because it's coming from a dog.

Bizarreness shouldn't be totally random. It works best if there's some pseudo-logic holding everything together. In the case of talking animals, we've all had experience with an animal who seemed practically human at one time or another. It's a small leap to imagine the animal walking on two legs and talking. This approach works with almost anything; you start with the ordinary and then exaggerate it until it becomes bizarre. That way you keep a thread back to the starting point.

By way of contrast, imagine a bowling ball that acts like a refrigerator. It's bizarre, but too illogical to be funny. It's totally random because there is no logical thread between the bowling ball and the refrigerator. It probably won't work for a joke.

But take a human resources director, then exaggerate the uncaring attitude and sadistic streak. What do you have? A cat, of course. That's why Mr. Catbert, the Evil Director of Human Resources, is a bizarreness that works.

Here are two bizarre concepts—sex and household appliances—that can be connected by a thin band of logic. Without the sliver of logic holding these two unrelated things in place, this wouldn't work.

RECOGNIZABILITY

Have you ever been in this situation? You pull up to a red light and there's no one else around for miles. You think about running the light. You look left, then right, then in your rearview mirror. No cops, no witnesses. It would be the perfect crime. You have miles of visibility in all directions. You smile inwardly, feeling evil. It's oddly satisfying. You think to yourself, "I'm bad."

Then the light turns green. You feel like a total weenie for sitting there like a ceramic frog in a coma while telling yourself how rebellious you are. You are not a rebel. You proceed cautiously into the intersection and turn right. Then you remember that in your state it's perfectly legal to turn right on a red light, so you didn't have to wait for the light anyway. You are a slow-witted nonrebel. And you signaled for the turn.

If you ever considered cheating on a red light, the situation I just described gave you the feeling I call "recognizability." You can easily put yourself in the situation and visualize it perfectly.

But visualizing a situation is not enough for humor purposes. You have to *feel* it. Let's say the story was about you stopping at a stoplight and then proceeding—nothing more. You can visualize that perfectly, but there is no emotional charge to the situation. You can't feel it in your gut. That situation wouldn't qualify as "recognizability" for the purpose of humor.

But let's add one element to the stoplight story to give it some juice. Let's say there's another driver behind you. You hesitate for just a moment after the light turns green, and the driver behind you honks his horn in a punitive way. You hate him, because he honked after you'd already started forward. It was an uncalled-for honk. Now the story qualifies as recognizability for humor, more so than in the first example. Start there and add another dimension to get humor.

The main pitfall with the recognizability dimension is that everyone has different experiences. It's hard to come up with a situation that everyone recognizes. Even the stoplight story is meaningless unless you drive a car. But there's a bigger pitfall if you go in the other direction—relying on universal themes like eating, romance, sleeping, and shopping. Those topics have been ridden hard by every funny person on earth. My advice is to write about the things that bug you personally, then hope some other people are feeling the same.

Here's an example that might seem unreal to some people, but it's not. Lots of people wrote to tell me their bosses made the same sort of request I show in this cartoon. For that group of unfortunates, this cartoon has recognizability, cleverness in the form of broken logic (I'll talk about that later), and a thin layer of meanness.

NAUGHTINESS

You might want to skip this section if you're easily offended.

The naughty dimension includes any topic you wouldn't want to mention to your mother. And I do mean specifically *your* mother, not mine. My mom isn't a good standard for naughtiness because she grew up on a dairy farm. Her chores included shoveling gigantic mounds of fecal matter, yanking those dangly things beneath cows, and arranging premarital sex for the chickens. In the same way that Eskimos have developed many words for snow, dairy farmers have also developed an extensive vocabulary for their environment. Farmers like to use everything they produce; that's why much of this colorful vocabulary pulls double duty as obscene expletives. It's important that farmers have a large reserve of expletives, because it's the sort of work that causes you to injure yourself several times per hour. No professional farmer wants to repeat his best material before noon.

The swearing on Mom's farm wasn't all work-related. Some was recreational, bordering on art. Grandfather's hobbies included going out to the barn at night and cursing at the cows until their milk tasted like grapefruit juice. My uncle reportedly knocked a squirrel out of a tree using nothing but carefully chosen words.

The point is, you'll have to use your own mom for the naughtiness test. Mine isn't easily shocked, unless you count her reaction when she reads this section. (Just kidding, Mom!)

Naughtiness is the easiest dimension to work with. You can take almost any ordinary situation, add something naughty to it, and it automatically seems bizarre or recognizable or mean. You get a second dimension of humor without any effort. That's why you see so much of it.

But naughtiness has risks. Many people believe that exposure to naughtiness is harmful to humans. You can test this for yourself by using identical twins who are under the impression that you invited them over for a party. Seal one twin in a soundproof container. Then tell the other twin this classic naughty joke:

Did you hear about the naked guy who ran through a crowded church? They caught him by the organ.

Observe and record the reaction of the twins. The twin in the   soundproof container will be beating on the wall yelling, "   !!!" which, roughly translated, is, "Help! Help! There's no air in this soundproof container!!!"

By contrast, the twin who had unprotected exposure to naughtiness will immediately become a crack-selling, ivory-poaching, jaywalking CPA. It won't be pretty. That's why it's wise to steer clear of the naughtiness dimension if you can. However, if you can't resist the siren song of naughtiness, there's a rule you *must* follow for your own protection:

Naughtiness Rule: The funnier the joke, the more
you can get away with.

Never use naughtiness in mixed company, unless your witticism is so funny that your audience will shoot tears of happiness out of their eyes with a velocity sufficient to powerwash a small bus. Any joke that falls short of that standard will make you lose respect in the eyes of everyone except your best friends, who, as you know, lost respect for you long ago. But if your naughtiness makes someone laugh, that person immediately abdicates his right to whine about it later. Humor can insulate you from criticism, at least a bit.

People will also tolerate far more naughtiness if they feel they had a choice about consuming it. For example, hardly anyone complains about romance novels. It's your own choice whether you want to read a naughty book or not. And you can't say you weren't warned. It's no secret what you'll find in a paperback titled *I Was Taken by a One-Eyed Pirate*. But if you put that type of naughtiness in the local newspaper, for example, readers will be caught off guard. They might bump into it inadvertently and feel violated. Imagine how shocking it would be to stumble on to this horoscope:

Scorpio

Oversexed Scorpios find their libidos in hyperdrive all week. If you've considered bestiality as a lifestyle—and what Scorpio hasn't?—this is a good time to grab the bull by the horns.

You don't have to go that far to get in trouble. Some newspapers wouldn't run the following *Dilbert* cartoons. One used the word "hiney" and the other used the colloquialism "sucked." These words wouldn't have raised an eyebrow in book form, but in the context of a newspaper, some editors felt that their communities couldn't handle the shock.

Here are a few jokes that appeared in my book, *Dogbert's Big Book of Etiquette*. No one complained. It's unlikely I could have gotten them published in newspapers.

Now, let's take an ordinary story from my real life—this morning, in fact—and show you how naughtiness can be added to a normal situation to make it funny. This true story already had built-in meanness, so all it needed was one more dimension. As you'll see, it isn't funny until the naughtiness is added. Here's a version of the story *without* naughtiness so you can see for yourself.

Boring Story with No Naughtiness

This morning I accidentally snapped myself with the elastic band of my pajamas. It hurt.

See what I mean? No humor. Now I will tell the same story, adding the naughty element. (This is a completely true story.)

Humorous Story with Naughtiness

I was wearing my red flannel pajamas, as is my custom this time of year. Nature called. For the benefit of the ladies, let me explain something about men's pajamas. There are two possible means of extracting one's manhood from red flannel pajamas, assuming we eliminate the foot holes as possibilities. The civilized way is to use the fly hole that is designed for that very purpose. But that can take more coordination than I have in the morning. The more efficient way is to simply grab the waistband and stretch it down. I chose that method. But being a bit klutzy, my hand slipped, allowing the elastic band to snap back in a vigorous fashion, making brisk contact with the two most sensitive parts of my body, which are not my eyeballs. This is not to say that my eyeballs were completely uninvolved, because they were actually bulging out and touching the wall in front of me at this point.

I jumped around for several minutes doing the *Nutcracker Waltz* while simultaneously singing the lost lyrics, which go something like this: "EEY-OWWW!!! OUCH OUCH OUCH AAAUU-UAAAAHHH!!!"

There, you see how that story didn't come alive until the naughtiness was added?

Naughtiness and meanness both work best when they are subtle or indirect. Here's an example where several mean and naughty elements are mixed together but each of them individually is somewhat subtle. And the reader is forced to reach his or her own conclusion about what the nickname might be.

Naughtiness and vulgarity often work when they happen offstage, in the imagination of the audience. Here's a good example. Had I shown the suggested gesture explicitly, the comic never would have been published.

You can get away with swearing when it would otherwise be offensive if you allude to the offending word but don't actually use it. In this way you can cause the bad word to register in the reader's head, exactly as you intended, but without committing the sin of writing or speaking it. I have no idea why transmitting a foul word indirectly is less offensive than transmitting it directly, but everyone acts like that's the case, so I don't question it. That's how I was able to get this cartoon published.

CLEVERNESS

As you might guess, the most challenging dimension is cleverness. It doesn't take much brain power to turn an ordinary situation into something mean or recognizable or bizarre or naughty. But cleverness requires some work.

I won't try to define cleverness too strictly. You know it when you see it. It's the thing that makes no sense but still makes sense. It's the thing you wish you'd thought of.

There are several classic paths to cleverness. These are the ones I use the most:

► Exaggeration

► Play on words

► Broken logic

Exaggeration: It's not enough to simply exaggerate something. That wouldn't be clever. There's nothing witty about saying, "This *Dilbert* book must have been written by the sexiest man alive!" That's nothing but a simple exaggeration. (And only barely that.) An exaggeration becomes clever when you take it to the next level. You have to exaggerate so incredibly that your audience is convinced that you could not exaggerate one bit further. Then you do, usually by adding an unexpected layer. That's the clever part.

Consider this cartoon:

It was a simple exaggeration that the boss would leave the building without telling the employees of the bomb threat. That wouldn't be enough to sell that joke. The unexpected layer—the thing that compounds his carelessness—is that he bought a lottery ticket. It's hard to explain why playing the lottery constitutes additional carelessness, but most people would see it that way, so it works.

Exaggeration is one of my favorite devices for writing *Dilbert*. I ask myself, If this is the worst that could happen, what would be even worse? Sometimes I have to suspend the laws of physics or the laws of Congress to make the exaggeration work.

Let's say you work for a company that doesn't care about you.

Normally, the worst thing they could do is fire you. Exaggerate one level more and the worst they could do is kill you. That's almost there. You need yet another level of exaggeration to make it work, as in this strip.

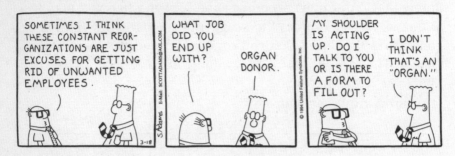

Here's another example, pulled from real life. I got an e-mail message from someone who complained of the photocopier being located in an employee's cubicle. It sounds like a comic exaggeration even though it's real. All I needed was a second level of exaggeration:

Play on Words: Puns are an easy way to be clever, but they don't qualify as funny on their own. A computer could generate puns, but they wouldn't make you laugh. The trick is to insert puns in situations where they would be rude, or mean, or naughty. It's the extra dimension that makes puns work.

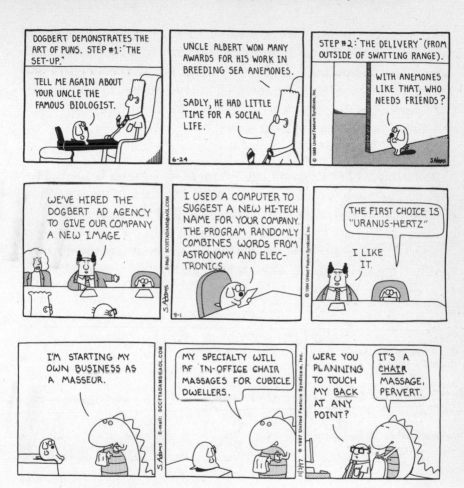

There are a few people—very few, actually—who enjoy pure, single-dimensional puns. The people in this group ask only that the puns are sufficiently complex and clever. Technically, this sort of pun worship is a form of appreciation more than it is a form of humor. I include myself in the pun-lover category. I can assure you it is a very lonely category.

Use puns sparingly, as no more than 10 percent of the general population appreciates them, and it's hard to know in advance who those people are. The only correlation I've noticed is that youngsters who have been accepted at Ivy League colleges usually like pure puns. In other words, "Use a pun, go to Yale."

See how lonely I am right now?

Broken Logic: The "Broken Logic" form of cleverness is the most difficult to create—and to me, the best. The trick is to take a normal situation and twist it just enough so that the logic is destroyed, yet not so much that the brain won't try to make sense of it. That's the secret: The brain has to automatically try to "fix" the unfixable, or else it's just random.

Here's an example.

In that example, the book is only *about* glue, not covered with glue. But your brain reflexively tries to make sense of it. At the moment of discomfort when your brain realizes it can't fix what's broken, it triggers a laugh response. I guess your brain doesn't know what else to do.

Here's another example. If you don't get this joke, the explanation follows.

Wally's last line about the missing pillow is a callback to a very old joke that goes like this:

> Last night I dreamed I was eating a giant marshmallow. This morning my pillow was gone.

If you've never heard that joke before, Wally's pillow reference makes no sense. I made a conscious choice to leave some readers on the curb with this one. But if you were familiar with the old marshmallow joke, the *Dilbert* cartoon put your brain in the uncomfortable position of resolving the broken logic between two entirely different jokes.

One of my favorite examples of broken logic was invented by a friend over dinner at a Chinese restaurant years ago. As was our tradition in this little foursome, we were examining the menu for spelling errors and typos before ordering. It became a contest. Each of us searched frantically for the next error, joyfully shouting the discoveries as we found them. Finally, with all spelling errors and typos seemingly identified, one friend pointed to a correctly spelled word and announced triumphantly, "Look! This one is pronounced wrong!"

COMBINING DIMENSIONS

Since many of the dimensions of humor are subjective, you can increase your odds of getting a laugh by using more than two dimensions. Here's one of my favorite multidimensional strips, using cuteness, meanness, bizarreness, cleverness and—for anyone who has ever worked with a consultant—some recognizability too. This cartoon gives almost anyone a reason to like it.

HUMOR EXERCISE

Now that you've read about all six of the dimensions, let's see how good you are at spotting them. Read the story below and see how many of the six elements you can find in this true story.

THE TRUE STORY OF THE SPIDER AND THE CAT

It was time for bed. I drank deeply from my glass of cool water, then placed it on the dresser in its usual spot. I snuggled under the covers and reached for the remote control that operates the bedroom lights. (Yes, I do have a remote control for the room lights. I spent many years around engineers, and some of it rubbed off. Too much, really.)

For some reason, that night the remote control was not on the nightstand where it belonged. No problem. I knew I would find it the next day. I hopped out of bed, turned off the lamps the old-fashioned way, and reclaimed my warm spot beneath the covers.

Things went fine until about 4:00 A.M., when I awoke and noticed the lights were on for some reason. It seemed odd, but I was too groggy to think about it. Realizing I was thirsty, I decided to take a gulp from my ever-ready glass of water. I always drink water when I wake up, because I sleep with my mouth open, so most of the moisture from my guts evaporates during the night. On cool nights, I can actually create a ground fog in the bedroom. Anyway, I've noticed that my guts work better when they're kept moist, so I add water often.

I take great pride in being able to find my water glass in total darkness. I know the number of steps from the bed, the height of the dresser, and the approximate location of the glass on the dresser. Sometimes I make beeping sounds and pretend I'm a bat using my sonar. The beeping doesn't help. I assume this is why bats never drink out of my water glass.

That night, no guesswork was needed, because the light was already on, for some mysterious reason. I picked up the glass, raised it to my lips, and came eye-to-tentacle with the biggest floating spider I have ever seen in my life.

I don't mean to exaggerate here. Imagine a Chihuahua with eight legs. Now imagine the Chihuahua being eaten by this spider. I'm talking about a *big* spider.

THAT MONSTER ALMOST WENT IN MY MOUTH!!!!
The only thing that saved me was the freak coincidence
that the lights had somehow been turned on in the middle
of the night. I discovered later that my cat Freddie had
waddled into the bedroom and used the misplaced remote
control for a pillow, accidentally turning on the light. He
was still snoozing on it when I discovered his heroism.

Freddie saved me!

As an optimist, I interpreted this as a stroke of incredible luck. The *one* time there is a spider in my water, my cat
turns on the lights and saves me. This is very high on the
coincidence scale. I believe it proves that either I am the
luckiest man on earth, or my cat Freddie has been watching reruns of *Lassie* and picking up a trick or two.

By way of contrast, my girlfriend, Pam, has a different
interpretation of this event. She cheerily pointed out that
in all likelihood I have consumed thousands of spiders and
never noticed it until the one time the lights were on.

THINKING IN OPPOSITES

If you have humor writer's block, a great way to get jump-started is
to imagine people and objects as the opposite of what they seem to be.

Take anything that makes sense and turn it inside out and

backwards just to see what it looks like. Sometimes you find gems. It's a good way to get your brain into creative mode.

TWO QUESTIONS TO ASK ABOUT ANYTHING

1.   What if it's not what it seems?

2.   What if it's the opposite of what it seems?

You'll be surprised how easily those two questions can free your thinking.

The method works best with characters. Take a normal character and make him the opposite of what his stereotype would suggest. Lots of times that creates problems for other characters, so you're halfway to Jokeville without even trying. Add a pinch of comedic exaggeration and you've got yourself some instant humor.

For example, you would expect a butler to be helpful and loyal. He would bring hot beverages on request. Now turn it around and exaggerate the opposite. Now you have a butler who despises his employer and tries to injure him as often as possible. He would spill hot beverages on his employer's genitalia, intentionally, several times a day. And then he would complain about being underpaid.

Movies and television shows are full of humorous opposites. In *The Wizard of Oz,* the lion is cowardly. In the movie *Liar Liar,* Jim Carrey plays a lawyer who can't lie. In the movie *Being There,* Peter Sellers is a dolt who becomes president. You can think of a hundred more.

HUMOROUS OPPOSITES

▶   Well-informed boss

▶   Murderous doctor

▶ Generous panhandler

▶ Small dog who wants to conquer the world

▶ Selfish angel

▶ Consultant who works for free

▶ Teacher who hates children

▶ Honest politician

▶ Vegetarian wolf

▶ Suicidal psychiatrist

Here's one of my favorite strips. It uses a simple opposite: a lazy beaver.

DIALOGUE TIPS

At some point in your career you will be asked to write humorous dialogue for one thing or another. It might be a skit for the department staff meeting, or a radio commercial for your business, or the comic strip you're creating in your cubicle while you steal time from the company. Whatever the reason, you can't avoid writing humor dialogue your whole life. Here are some tips to help you do it well.

Dialogue Tip 1: The average person is ignorant, self-absorbed, and generally evil. Keep that in mind when you're writing humorous dialogue.

If you write dialogue where every character is acting with an exaggerated sense of self-interest, sprinkled with a bit of ignorance, your audience will say to you later, "That was so realistic." The secret to realism is selfishness. The more the better. Slather it on. You can't exaggerate selfishness so much that it appears unrealistic.

Dialogue Tip 2: Real people rarely talk in a question-and-answer format. When someone asks a question, the other person normally responds in one of these ways:

1. *He answers the wrong question intentionally, just to be annoying.*
2. *He ignores the question and talks about something related to himself.*
3. *He makes a joke.*
4. *He wonders aloud how this possibly matters to him.*
5. *He proves by his response that he is too dumb to understand the question.*
6. *He gets offended by the question.*

WRITING STYLE

Humor can't survive complicated sentences. Use the same writing style for humor as you use for good business writing. I don't mean the kind of business writing that you see from your co-workers, filled with incomprehensible nonwords. I mean the kind of business writing that is simple and to the point. It's the kind of business writing you would learn if you took a class called Business Writing. And you should take one, whether you plan to be funny or not. After the course, your written ideas will seem more brilliant and no one will know why. (I discovered that phenomenon after taking a business-writing class. Seriously, it's one of the best things you can do for your career.)

I can't teach you good business writing in this book, but two points are worth mentioning because they are essential to humor.

RULE 1: AVOID INDIRECT SENTENCES

INDIRECT SENTENCE
The log was eaten by a beaver.

DIRECT SENTENCE
A beaver ate the log.

Both sentences say the same thing, but your brain processes the direct sentence faster. It might seem like an insignificant difference, but I've never seen successful humor that used indirect sentences.

RULE 2: KEEP IT SIMPLE. FORGET ABOUT ACCURACY

No one remembers the details of what you say. Get rid of your sentence modifiers. Sometimes you can make an ordinary insight sound funny by simply stripping out the modifiers. Here's an example:

COMPLICATED VERSION (NOT FUNNY)
Often, in the course of normal life, very bad things

can happen to you for no reason at all. It is advisable that you not dwell overlong upon it.

SIMPLE VERSION (FUNNY)
Shit happens.

Here's a good example of a cartoon that would be ruined by adding any clarifying words.

HONESTY IS FUNNY

You can make an ordinary situation funny by substituting honesty where, ordinarily, people would lie or avoid saying anything. Honesty in social situations is so rare that it automatically qualifies as bizarre. And it's usually cruel too. You get two of the six dimensions of humor—bizarre and mean—without much effort. I use this method often, as in this example.

BRAINSTORMING

Brainstorming got its name from a method that was developed during the Dark Ages. The technique involved removing the brains of smart people and leaving them out in a storm. The storm-washed brains would then be beaten against flat stones and hung out to dry. Later they would be ironed to get the crevices out. After the freshly laundered brains were sewn back into their original skulls, the smart people would be expected to come up with good ideas. If they didn't, it was proof they were witches.

This process has lost favor everywhere except in England, where it was credited over the years with creating such good ideas as warm beer, overtaxing the American colonies, Twiggy, and pissing off the Irish.

Everywhere else, the meaning of brainstorming changed over time. Now it refers to a process where you take a group of people who have bad ideas and make them sit in the same room. Consultants have discovered that when you take people with bad ideas and clump them together, you get—and this is the amazing part—a large clump of bad ideas. Some of those ideas are much worse than others. If you sit in a brainstorming session long enough, the least putrid ideas start to sound quite brilliant. But that's not the only benefit of the technique.

When you get a lot of bad ideas in one place, they start to morph into new and exciting bad ideas. Here are some examples of how simple bad ideas can bind to become hybrid, complex bad ideas.

Simple Bad Idea	Hybrid Bad Idea
Give employees monogrammed pencils instead of bonuses . . .	. . . then insist that employees change names so they all have the same initials.

Simple Bad Idea	Hybrid Bad Idea
Invent a beer can with a motorized straw for quicker drinking . . .	. . . equipped with an adapter for the car lighter.

Instead of brainstorming with other people, I recommend brainstorming with yourself. It's faster, and you don't have to keep a straight face when your co-workers exhibit the type of brilliance that gives all mammals a bad name. When you brainstorm alone, all you lose is the knowledge and viewpoints of other people—and that's something you can learn to fake with very little effort.

THINKING CREATIVELY

One of the questions I'm most often asked is "How do you think up a new cartoon idea every day?" Like most things in life, there are some tricks to it. If you know the tricks, it's not as hard as it might seem. I'll tell you how I approach creativity. I doubt that one creative method works for everyone, but it will give you something new to try. Judge for yourself.

The way I look at it, creativity is a matter of pushing bad ideas out of your mind so new ones can flow in. The active part of the process—the part you can develop with practice—is the flushing of bad ideas from your head to make room for new ones.

Getting rid of bad ideas is less scary than trying to create something from nothing. "Creating" is not the sort of mental process anyone can understand or manage in a direct sense. You have to go at it indirectly. That's why it's useful to think of creativity backward—as a process of eliminating bad ideas.

Unless you're a monk with ten years of meditation training, your mind isn't capable of being empty, even for a moment. As soon as one thought leaves, another takes its place. If the new thought isn't good enough for your purposes, don't dwell on it. Just release it. Try to increase the number of ideas you evaluate per minute. The more ideas you evaluate, the better your odds of hitting a winner. Use the odds to your advantage.

The best and quickest way to evaluate your ideas is to use your gut instead of your common sense. I mean that literally. Great ideas have an immediate physical impact on your body. If you're trying to create humor, your body will laugh when the right idea crosses your mind. If you're trying to create an idea with emotional impact, your body will tense up or cry or shake when you think of a winning idea. I've even noticed that my body responds physically to ideas that don't directly involve an emotion, such as a good business idea. (Those make me tingle.)

Technically, your brain is still doing all the evaluating, not your digestive system. But when it comes to creativity, your brain isn't so good at signaling its preferences directly. You have to pick up the messages indirectly, in your muscles and glands and circulatory system.

Listening to your body instead of your brain is against your nature, so it takes practice. It's tempting to give each of your ideas a thorough rational analysis—weighing the pros and the cons—before going to the next. And it's tempting to hold on to an idea that doesn't work, in the hope that further analysis will discover it wasn't such a bad idea after all. Those are normal impulses. You won't learn to trust your gut to make the quick filtering decisions until you've created a good track record for yourself.

Your personality is probably the biggest factor in whether you're able to release ideas quickly. Some people are natural collectors. They hold on to things reflexively. They keep mementos, they take photographs, they dwell on past relationships. My personality is the opposite extreme. I live almost entirely in the next moment. I don't own a camera. I can't watch a movie twice no matter how much I liked it the first time. For me, forgetting an idea is natural and easy most of the time. Yet I still have to remind myself to let go once in a while. If you're the kind of person who never throws anything away, you might have a hard time with this technique.

The surest sign of a bad idea is one that passes the brain test but not the gut test. An idea that "makes sense" is the hardest to release. It's especially hard to release if you've spent some time evaluating it. You become invested. The worst thing you can do with that sort of idea is share it with others. They too will see the sense of it and tell you it's a good idea. Bad ideas that make sense start to get their own weight if you don't banish them right away.

The one big problem I've noticed from listening to my gut is that sometimes an idea will be scary. Then the fear reaction will mask any other physical reaction. This wouldn't be such a big problem except that the ideas that are the scariest (at least in terms of potential embarrassment) are so often the best ones. This true story is a good example.

RAY MEBERT—EXPERT CONSULTANT

I got a call from Tia O'Brien, a freelance writer on assignment for the *San Jose Mercury News*. She had been asked to do a story about me in my role as *Dilbert* cartoonist. The newspaper asked her to approach it from an angle that was fresh and interesting. We discussed some ideas over the phone until we came up with the most frighteningly embarrassing plan of my entire life. Naturally, Tia liked that plan, since it would make a good story no matter how it worked out. The plan was this: I would be disguised by a professional makeup artist and try to pass myself off as a world-class consultant for a major company. Tia would come along as my "assistant." I would see how far I could yank the chains of the executives before they tarred and feathered me.

Tia worked her contacts in the industry and found an accomplice with a sense of fun and adventure: Pierluigi Zappacosta (yes, that's his actual name), co-founder and then vice chairman of Logitech International. (They make computer mice and other input devices.) Pierluigi agreed to call the senior staff together to meet with the famous consultant, code-named "Ray Mebert."* I had two specific goals for the meeting:

1. Lead the executives into creating the longest, most useless, buzzword-heavy mission statement on earth.

2. Get volunteers to agree to put the mission statement to music.

As the makeup artist applied my large puffy brunette wig and my fake mustache that morning, I could feel my various guts arguing with one another about the best way to stop me from doing this. If my intended victims recognized the bad disguise, or if they saw through my act, I would waste a lot of people's time that day. If I yanked their chains too hard, I would find myself in a room full of very angry executives. Tension was high. Tia decided to raise the stakes by bringing a film crew to record the action. Our cover story for the executives was that the video would be made available to the rest of the employees later to get "buy-in."

The executives filed in and took their places around a large conference table. Pierluigi introduced me, then sat down to play his part in the prank. He was to nod approvingly, no matter what I

---

*If a dog is a Dogbert and a cat is a Catbert and a Rat is a Ratbert, I figured I must be a Mebert. But we used the French pronunciation.

said. I started by telling the group a little about my background—my fictitious Harvard MBA, my fictitious experience consulting for several failed endeavors, and most notably my experience on the "Taste Bright" project at Procter & Gamble. I explained that while working at P&G I had discovered through research that people often tasted the detergents and cleansers before using them. My job was to improve the taste of all the soap products. There were murmurs of approval at this "out of box" thinking.

Next, I went to the easel, where I drew a diagram of three rings intersecting and labeled it the "Mission Triad." The circles were labeled: Message, Authority, and Linguistics. The intersection was what I called "The Buy-in Zone." It was all nonsense, but the kind of nonsense that is so pervasive in corporate settings that no one openly questions it. The group waited politely to see if any content would emerge.

Within an hour I managed to lead the executives into creating this mission statement:

Mission Statement

The New Ventures Mission is to scout profitable growth opportunities in relationships, both internally and externally, in emerging, mission-inclusive markets, and explore new paradigms and then filter and communicate and evangelize the findings.

By this time, my credibility and charisma were high enough to ask for their help in putting the mission statement to music. I explained that although this might seem silly on the surface, there is a wealth of evidence that people can remember words more easily if they are put to music. Two executives confessed to having musical talent, and—since they were team players—they agreed to take on the task of the musical mission statement. Mercifully, I ripped off the wig and mustache and revealed my true identity. The shock soon turned to laughter and a good time was had by all. Tia turned the incident into a feature story that got a lot of attention, and no one has tried to kill me yet. That outcome was as good as it could have been. Fortunately for me, Logitech is a confident company with a good sense of humor. (I'm certain I would have gotten the same results at any company on earth, except for maybe the good-sense-of-humor part.)

Had I listened to my gut, I probably wouldn't have undertaken this creative venture. What I've learned over time is that the fear response often comes with the best ideas. If your creative idea doesn't bring with it some risk of embarrassment, it probably isn't too special. When it comes to creativity, fear can be a good signal, as long as it's only fear of embarrassment.

Mild-mannered cartoonist
Scott Adams

Scott Adams disguised as
super consultant Ray Mebert

(Both photos by Richard Hernandez/*San Jose Mercury News*)

Consultant Ray Mebert works his magic
(Richard Hernandez/*San Jose Mercury News*)

THE MIRACLE OF CREATIVE VOLUME

Most people would be embarrassed to fail 80 percent of the time. Not me. I call that a good week. If I can make someone laugh at one *Dilbert* strip out of five, I know I will be forgiven for the next four. There's a honeymoon effect with humor, as there is with most forms of creativity. Learn to exploit it.

I know people who will make one terrific suggestion to a new boss and then get discouraged when the suggestion is shot down. Or worse, they'll keep hammering at their bosses with the same doomed suggestions, thinking that persistence will pay off. That is a bad strategy.

A better approach is to create *more* ideas that your boss hates. Try twenty more ideas. Ignore the rejections. Eventually, by pure accident, you'll hit an idea that your boss likes. You won't be remembered as the person who had nineteen **bad** ideas. You'll be the employee who had the one **good** idea. Bad ideas that aren't implemented are quickly forgotten.

Try twenty more ideas. If you get lucky a second time, you'll be known as the employee who is full of good ideas, despite your 95 percent failure rate. You might even be able to drag out that first doomed idea and try it again, this time under the halo of your spectacular track record.

Recently I attended an event where a well-known businessman was giving a talk. A member of the audience was acquainted with someone who once served on the board of directors with this businessman. He told me that the businessman was notorious for bringing ten new ideas to every meeting, of which at least nine were incredibly bad. The businessman was Ted Turner, billionaire founder of CNN.

Quiz 1: Name any one of Ted Turner's *bad* ideas.

Quiz 2: What makes you so sure *any* of his ideas
were bad?

If you're going to create, create a lot. Creativity is not like playing the slot machines, where failure to win means you go home broke. With creativity, if you don't win, you're usually no worse off than if you hadn't played. Creativity has very few downsides, except one: critics.

9

Handling Criticism

When I was a kid, I saw a movie where everyone on earth turned into a dangerous zombie except one guy. Every night the zombies would surround his house and try to turn him into a zombie too. Being creative is exactly like being that guy. If you create anything new—even if it's only an idea—the zombies (hereafter referred to as critics) will surround your office or home and try to recruit you into their cult of normalcy. The critics can effectively neutralize any happiness you get from your creativity.

Here's a simple recipe for handling critics:

RECIPE FOR HANDLING A CRITIC

Ingredients: Four cloves of garlic, one small cross, and one bag of fresh parsley

Eat the four cloves of garlic. Hold the small cross directly in front of the critic and say, "Look what I just made. Do you like it?" The critic will be unable to move until he has pointed out the flaws in your design. Breathe normally until you hear the thud of the critic's skull against the floor. Eat the bag of parsley to hide the murder weapon.

Depending on your ethical preferences, that method might not be acceptable to you. For example, some people are morally opposed to eating parsley. If you're one of them, you'll need other strategies. But first you must identify what sort of critic you are dealing with. Critics fall into these four categories:

TYPES OF CRITICS

1. People who reflexively criticize any idea (contrarians)

2. People who enjoy making you suffer (sadists)

3. People who are angry for no good reason (nuts)

4. People with valid criticisms (bastards)

CONTRARIAN CRITICS

Contrarians are the easiest types of critics to deal with. They're motivated by an obsessive need to demonstrate their brilliance at your expense. For the contrarian, there is no such thing as a good idea that comes from someone else. If you say puppies are fun, the contrarian will say they eat your slippers. If you say sunny days make you feel good, he'll say the sun gives you wrinkles.

Fortunately for you, the contrarian's predictability is his downfall. I once worked with a contrarian engineer. I needed his approval for all plans that had an impact on his area. After the tenth consecutive encounter in which he ripped my ideas to bits, I realized he was a compulsive contrarian, and not merely a cantankerous pessimist. Thereafter, I introduced all new plans to him by first proclaiming them to be hideously expensive and physically impossible. This forced him to provide a vigorous defense of my idea followed by enthusiastic approval. When I moved to a new job and no longer needed him alive, I told him it was impossible for him to hold his breath for thirty minutes. The police ruled it a justifiable suicide.*

---

*Not really, but don't you wish it were that easy?

SADISTIC CRITICS

Sadistic critics are the hardest to deal with, especially at work, because you can't escape them. There's no point in reasoning with sadists because they're only in it for the pleasure of making you feel bad. If you show any weakness, it will only encourage them to do it again. That's why I recommend that you respond to the sadistic critic using a strategy that resembles demonic possession. Start by asking yourself, What would Satan do in this situation? Then go with it. If you can spin your head around and spew vomit, that will make a lasting impression on anyone else who was thinking of taking a run at you. The goal is to train all the sadists in your office so that they focus their evil somewhere else.

Sadist: Your idea is ill-conceived and doomed.

You: You short-sighted, pompous bag of monkey crap. Your breath smells like the rotting flesh of a thousand corpses!! I'll dance on your grave when my brilliant idea makes billions of dollars! BUWAHHAHAHA!!!

If the sadist complains about your verbal assault, look surprised and say, "Oh . . . I thought that's what we were doing." Obviously the demonic-possession strategy can have no productive business outcome. But it might make you feel better, and that is its own reward.

PEOPLE WHO ARE ANGRY FOR NO GOOD REASON

When you create anything—especially humor—there's a good chance that people will get angry for no good reason. When people get mad for no reason, you will be branded "insensitive."

For example, literally two minutes ago, I got a complaint from someone who was disturbed about this cartoon. I can't figure out why.

I've tried being sensitive to the feelings of other people, but there are six billion other people stomping around the planet, and each one is completely different. My brain is barely big enough to know what my own body is feeling. I mean, sometimes when I get an itch, I scratch three different body parts before I find it. And sometimes I think I'm tired, then I eat a snack, and suddenly I'm not tired anymore. Apparently, I can't even tell the difference between being tired and being hungry. If I'm confused about the feelings in my own body, there's no hope for me to know what anyone else is feeling. Yet society expects me to try. So most of the time I have to fake being sensitive.

Fortunately for me, I've offended so many people in my career that I've learned to recognize patterns that are likely to get me in trouble. That's why I wrote this chapter. It's for people who are hopelessly insensitive but who haven't yet insulted enough people to recognize the patterns.

In this chapter, I'll show you some of the angry responses I've gotten to *Dilbert* comics—ones that might surprise you—so you can see the kinds of things that get people all worked up. Once you recognize the patterns that offend people, you'll be able to steer clear of them, thus giving the false impression that you are sensitive. In time, you'll be able to leverage that false impression into undeserved respect, shallow friendships, and a deep sense of your own moral superiority.

The next section is interactive. See if you can guess who was offended by this cartoon.

The biggest problem was my timing. It turned out to be a particularly bad week to make jokes about nuns. The cartoon was published at the same time Mother Teresa was being buried. (My cartoons are drawn months in advance. I usually don't know which ones are running on any given day.)

The Mother Teresa connection wasn't the only problem. Take a look at the mail I got that week and see how many of the complaints you would have anticipated.

From: [name withheld]
To: scottadams@aol.com

I have enjoyed "Dilbert" since it first appeared in my paper. I must say, however, that I'm very disappointed in, and offended by, the story line currently running in the *Chicago Tribune*. Many people I know must travel by air as part of their job and I fail to see the humor or cause for celebration of the fact that someone may have been lost in an airplane crash. In fact, I think it's about as tasteless as you can get—whether the crash actually happened or not. Let's get on to a new story line!

From: [name withheld]
To: scottadams@aol.com

On the day that the world mourns the passing of Sister Teresa and she is honored in Calcutta, we feel it is in very poor taste that you use nuns as a source of humor. It is the timing rather than the content.

You and your publisher should have adjusted the release to not coincide with the funeral. We often enjoy your brand of humor. This time you have overstepped the bounds.

From: [name withheld]
To: scottadams@aol.com

Your cartoon today was extremely insulting to all people whose loved ones have been involved in aircraft accidents. In addition, it was thoughtless to all religious nuns. At a time when the world is mourning Mother Teresa's death, it seemed heartless and ill-timed. You owe the world an apology.

From: [name withheld]
To: scottadams@aol.com

Let me begin by stating that I usually find your comic strip quite amusing. (I'll bet you're just waiting for the "however" well, here it is . . .) HOWEVER, the strip that was in print on 9-13-97 was quite distasteful. Given the recent death of Mother Teresa, this was obscene. Whether this strip was written before Mother Teresa's death is immaterial; you managed to make fun of the only two groups that are still politically correct to publicly chastise—Catholics and fat people.

You were correct that nuns don't do a lot of aerobics; they spend their time praying, teaching, and ministering to others. One would think that that would exclude them from being the brunt of such a cruel joke.

Please do not reply with rationalizations or justifications for your actions—they may help you sleep at night, but I do not have time to read them.

I pray that you see the inappropriateness of this comic and regret having written it.

The worst thing you can do when accused of being insensitive is to defend yourself with clever arguments. For example, I could argue that nuns would be delighted to go to heaven. And nuns would be glad to save a person's life. For a nun, my cartoon described a perfect day. If you look at it logically, my comic was really an inspirational story with a happy ending. Sure, I *could* make that argument, but I won't, because I've learned that angry people are immune to my flawless logic. For some reason, people just get upset when you demonstrate how clever you are.

On occasion, I have responded to charges of insensitivity by pointing out how insensitive it is for anyone to accuse me of insensitivity without fully understanding why I act the way I do. Then I express my hope that one day, insensitive people like me will be loved for what we are, not stereotyped. If you're thinking of trying that approach, I can tell you that it fails every time.

There is only one effective response when accused of insensitivity: Accuse your accuser of a sin called political correctness. Political correctness is a totally meaningless phrase, similar to "insensitivity." Neither has any useful meaning because they both describe every person on earth. Realistically, everyone whines when his or her own demographic group is maligned. We're all politically correct. So it's like accusing a dog of having hair on its body. Yet many people are so bothered by the label "politically correct" that they will withdraw their accusations of insensitivity and apologize for being so testy. This is another case of stupidity triumphing over stupidity. It shouldn't work, but it does. You might as well take advantage of it.

Let's look at another strip that I thought was harmless when I created it. See if you can identify the offensive element.

Several readers wrote to call me a "white racist pig," and other words to that effect, because of the reference to South Korea. I *could* argue that it's insensitive for anyone to call me white, because I have 1/128th Native American blood. That's not enough to open my own gambling casino, but it isn't exactly "white" either. Unfortunately, as you've learned from the prior example, that argument would only make my accusers angrier. And the Native Americans and casino operators wouldn't be too pleased either. That's why I would *not* make that argument.

Here's a comic that caused a minor firestorm. See if you can guess why.

If you guessed that autograph collectors complained because I suggested they are gullible, you'd be wrong. I didn't hear a peep. I was surprised.

But autograph *dealers* complained strenuously. Several wrote to tell me that they did **not** sell forgeries. One dealer said he always provides a signed certificate of authenticity to prove his signed memorabilia are not fake. (Really, he said that.)

The angriest readers were the ones who wrote to say I was "irreverent" and "insulting" to Jesus Christ. Some said I "mocked" religion.

I *could* have made the following argument: If Jesus saw that comic, would he be offended? Or would he laugh, ask for the original, and go off and save souls? I think he'd laugh heartily and give me a couple of backstage passes to his next sermon. Maybe he'd ask for the original. (Unless he was more of a *Ziggy* fan.) My argument, if I were foolish enough to make one, would rhetorically ask, shouldn't the followers of Jesus have the same priorities that he does? Isn't that pretty much the point?

Wisely, I decided *not* to make that argument.

Have you found the pattern of what makes people angry? It doesn't matter what you *say* about a topic, it only matters what context you put it in. I call it the problem of "proximity." It's the most important concept you must understand in order to pretend you are sensitive.

The proximity problem happens when you put two incompatible concepts in the same setting. In the nun comic, the death of Mother Teresa was too recent. Even though the cartoon had nothing to do with Mother Teresa, the proximity exacerbated its offensiveness.

In the comic about South Korea, I mentioned the country in the middle of a cartoon that involved unethical behavior, cruelty, ignorance, and stupidity. It didn't matter that none of those negative traits were ascribed to South Koreans. The proximity problem blended the country and the unrelated negatives all together in people's perception.

In the sports memorabilia cartoon, I made the mistake of including Jesus in a cartoon that addressed unscrupulous behavior and gullibility. I wasn't implicating Jesus in anything negative, but I failed to keep him at a safe distance from it. People were angry but couldn't easily explain why. It was a pure proximity problem.

My biggest proximity mistake was a series of *Dilbert* strips where Wally orders a mail-order bride from the mythical land of Elbonia.

People saw much symbolism in that cartoon. The problem is that it wasn't intended to be a symbolic cartoon. In my mind, the pig was just a pig, albeit a talking pig. It was not a metaphor for anything. I thought it would be funny if, instead of getting a human bride, Wally got ripped off by the mail-order company and got a nonhuman bride. To me, it was a clever indictment of the mail-order industry.

Unfortunately, many people found hidden messages in that cartoon. Women flamed me for suggesting that all women are pigs. People who married mail-order brides flamed me for suggesting their wives were pigs. Mail-order bride companies flamed me for suggesting their clients are pigs. But my favorite letter from the realm of the bizarre was this one:

Dear Mr. Scott Adams,

I have been reading your cartoon *Dilbert* for many years. Could you tell me the meaning of the 1/9/97 cartoon that appeared in the *Dallas Morning News*? Is it talking down to people in general? Or is it talking about the Black slang language Ebonics? I looked up the Internet Directory of Countries in the world and could not find Elbonia. What does the low expectations mean? And is the snout talking about African-American facial features versus European facial features?

As your loyal reader, I anxiously await your reply.
[name omitted]

I never answered that letter, so I would like to take the opportunity to do it here:

Dear [name omitted]

WHAT THE HELL IS WRONG WITH YOU????!!!!

Sincerely,
Scott Adams

The key to faking sensitivity is to abandon any hope that other people will react rationally to what you say and do. No one is rational about anything he cares about. I'm not. You're not. If you want to avoid being called insensitive, avoid the proximity problem and you will eliminate 80 percent of all appearances of insensitivity.

But no matter how careful you are, there are always surprises. In my book *The Dilbert Future* I suggested that people who write down their goals every day get better results than those who don't. Can you see any problem with that? Several people did. Here's a typical one.

From:[name withheld]
To: scottadams@aol.com

I was disappointed about your promotion of the use of the affirmations technique. The "power" you are tapping into is just another element of the New Age panorama, and its workings are manipulated not by you, but by the enemy of our souls. He'd have you believe you are enabling events to occur while all along you are just being given what you want so as to keep you from beholding the Savior of the world, Jesus Christ. The earth and all things in it belong to God, and we are not here to get whatever things we desire. We are here to glorify God in whatever we do. He is reality.

VALID CRITICISM

The worst type of criticism is the kind that is valid. If you are the recipient of valid criticisms you will lose the love and respect that you have worked so hard to earn. Fortunately, you can make up the gap by using trickery to gain additional love and respect that you don't deserve. Let these two cartoons be your guide.

▶ THE TROUBLE WITH NORMAN

Critics can be very annoying when they're right. But they're much worse when they're wrong. Your first reaction might be to hunt them down, strap powerful explosives to their bodies, then videotape the explosion to use later as a screensaver for your computer. But this is illegal in almost every state, except Texas, where you can get away with it if you claim the critic was trying to break into your house. If you don't live in Texas, I recommend that you do what I do: Use your critics for personal gain. This chapter can serve as your model.

Media critic Norman Solomon recently wrote a book called *The Trouble with Dilbert.* It was a scholarly analysis of the danger that the *Dilbert* comic strip poses to civilization. Special attention was given to a discussion of the author's greed, cynicism, and hypocrisy. This hurt me, because in my heart I know I am only greedy and cynical.

When Solomon's book hit the shelves, the media flocked to the story, always eager to find an angle where "man bites Dogbert."

In a widely published AP story, reporter Michael Hill summarized Solomon's complaints in a way that makes it unnecessary for you to read the actual book:

1. *Dilbert* pokes fun at ordinary workers and middle management, as if it's totally their fault workplaces are inefficient.

2. In an era of job cuts and corporate abuses, *Dilbert* lets upper management off the hook.

3. Adams is sympathetic to corporate downsizing tactics.

4. Adams is cynically making scads of money by licensing his creations to anyone.

5. Instead of being a weapon against mind-numbing corporate blather, *Dilbert* is a tool for propagating more of it.

If you're old enough, you might remember the late Gilda Radner's character on *Saturday Night Live*. She played a confused woman—"Emily Litella"—who would hear something incorrectly and launch into a lengthy and emotional monologue against the perceived injustice. When later informed that the real problem is that she misheard something, she ended her act with an embarrassed "Never mind." Norman is in the same situation, as far as I can tell.

It all started when a reporter asked me this question: "Scott, since you constantly attack corporate downsizing in your books and your comic strip, can you think of anything that is *good* about downsizing?"

That's when I made the biggest media blunder of my life: I gave an unbiased opinion. (Mentally insert the sound of Homer Simpson saying, "DOH!") I answered by saying that companies lowered expenses by downsizing. They became more competitive and their stock prices went up. If you're a stockholder, those things are good for you. I rounded out my answer with the observation that at Pacific Bell, my old employer, the bureaucracy decreased as the number of useless managers declined.

I didn't address the obvious bad aspects of downsizing—the disruption of lives, the emotional devastation, the constant fear, and the increased workload of the survivors. The context of the question was that everyone knows that stuff. It's what I talk about all the time in *Dilbert*.

My comments on the "benefits of downsizing" made it into print.

Norman saw my quote in a publication and called me to ask if I had really said that downsizing has benefits. I confirmed my quotes. (DOH! again.) I didn't realize that by now the original context—my continuous writing about the hideous effects of downsizing on employees—had already evaporated. Suddenly I was—to use Norman's words—"in favor of downsizing."

Armed with this valuable piece of misinformation, all the pieces fell into place for Norman: The author of *Dilbert* was evidently a tool of the capitalist pigs who oppress the working class. The most damning evidence was that many large companies pay for *Dilbert*-related activities (licensing, speaking, etc.). I was taking money from the enemy! Apparently this money trail set me apart from all the other published cartoonists who—and this is not widely known—get all of their compensation by breaking into parking meters.

Advice to Norman: Many newspapers, magazines, and book publishers are large corporations. Be sure to avoid taking their money as you pursue your writing career. Otherwise you will lose your credibility.

Norman and his publisher issued a press release and created a media campaign to publicize the anti-*Dilbert* book. Suddenly my phone was ringing and reporters wanted to know my response to the charges. Where there's smoke there must be fire, they reasoned. This controversy must be important because it's in an actual book! For the media, anyone who is opposed to anything is news.

I found myself on the defensive. But I couldn't figure out exactly what I was defending. I've spent so much time around engineers and economics majors that I couldn't see the world the way the journalism majors in the media painted it. For example, it seems to me that the ultimate victory in life is to mock large corporations and have them pay me to do it while everyone watches. To me, that's funny. Maybe even ironic. To the media, that is blatant hypocrisy.

My philosophy is very consistent. For example, if I were attacked by a mugger and somehow I managed to kill him in self-defense, I'd take his wallet before I left the crime scene. Some people would call this hypocritical. I call it good economics. And funny. Maybe even ironic.

Obviously it wouldn't make sense to address Norman's points in my normal rational way, since we have different views of what is rational. Instead, I give you an imaginary interview between Dogbert and Norman Solomon. You could say that all of the quotes attributed to Norman here are total fabrications. But I prefer to think of it as taking his own words out of context. That's what critics do, so it would be hypocritical for him to complain. Besides, there's a good chance that Norman has used all of these words at one time or another, admittedly not in this particular sequence. I'll do my best to "edit" them in a way that captures the intellectual integrity of his argument.

DOGBERT VERSUS SOLOMON

Dogbert: Thank you for agreeing to this interview, Mr. Solomon.

Norman: I didn't agree to it. I'm a fabrication so you won't get sued for libel.

Dogbert: My first question is, what's up with your hair?

Norman: My hair?

Dogbert: Yeah. I mean, your head looks like a mushroom with fur. Do you own a mirror?

Norman: I don't see what that has to do with anything.

Dogbert: Well, I noticed you didn't sell many copies of your book.

Norman: So?

Dogbert: Have you considered renting your head out as a pot scrubber for large hotels?

Norman: Are you going to ask me any questions about my provocative anti-*Dilbert* book?

Dogbert: Fair enough. So, you accuse Mr. Adams of favoring downsizing?

Norman: That's right. Mr. Adams is a cynical man. Downsizing is bad.

Dogbert: What is the alternative to downsizing that you favor?

Norman: Alternative?

Dogbert: Does it start with a "C" and end with the fall of the Iron Curtain?

Norman: Companies should not be able to hire and fire people just to increase profits for greedy owners!

Dogbert: Can you think of any economies that have tried it your way? (Hint: Albania)

Norman: Okay, sometimes it might be necessary to downsize people. But I object to the *way* it's done.

Dogbert: So, then you are in complete agreement with Mr. Adams—one of the most vocal critics of downsizing tactics on the planet earth?

Norman: No, no. That's different. Mr. Adams is only saying bad things about downsizing so he can make money from people. He's obviously cynical about it because he works with big corporations.

Dogbert: Didn't I see you on MSNBC promoting your book?

Norman: So?

Dogbert: Do you know who owns MSNBC?

Norman: I assumed it was the Multiple Sclerosis people. Is that wrong?

Dogbert: You imply that Mr. Adams is anti-worker because he doesn't spend as much time criticizing senior management as he could.

Norman: Yes, that's a logical conclusion based on the facts.

Dogbert: Have you ever published any criticisms of teen pregnancy?

Norman: What's that got to do with anything?

Dogbert: Obviously you're in favor of teen pregnancy. Otherwise you would be speaking out against it right now instead of having this interview.

Norman: Stop it! I refuse to do any more of this fictitious interview!

Norman didn't end his campaign against *Dilbert* with his worst-selling book. He updated his case with an article on the Disgruntled Website in December of 1997, in which he accused me of the following heinous crimes against humanity:

ALLEGED CRIMES OF SCOTT ADAMS

1. Opposing inefficiency

2. Making money

These crimes don't look so bad when they're summarized. But due to the fact that squirrels live in Norman Solomon's skull, the wording of his article made me hate myself when I read it. I could hardly believe what kind of person I had become. Norman knows how to turn a phrase. Here's a quote in which he savages my preference for efficiency:

> During the mid-1990's, *Dilbert* came to function as a stealth weapon against workers. After all, bosses cracking whips are not apt to have much credibility. But a clever satire of inefficiency can go where no whip-cracking is able to penetrate.

If Norman is opposed to people who favor efficiency, it follows logically that he is in favor of inefficiency. That sort of philosophy must make his life very difficult. No wonder he's grumpy. I'm wondering how he gets around town. Efficiency-loving people like me would probably take a car, or perhaps even a bicycle. But Norman is on record in favor of inefficiency. So I'm guessing he glues thousands of hummingbirds to his body and hopes they all fly in the same direction.

I realize that by the time you read this chapter, Norman Solomon may have shed his human "container" to follow a comet. So the debate may have ended on its own. But I couldn't resist the opportunity to use Norman for my own capitalist purposes here. I think it's funny. Maybe even ironic. With any luck, he'll write a sequel.

10

The Downside of Success

If you plan to use the tips in this book to amass wealth and fame, make sure you know what you're getting into. It's not as glamorous as you might think. As a public service, I will describe my own life—a typical day in the life of a semifamous cartoonist. Then you can decide for yourself whether fame and fortune are for you.

First, some background. I share a home with my longtime girl-friend, Pam. Pam is a vice president of a technology company and has never once been the source of humor for a *Dilbert* cartoon, as far as she knows.

One of Pam's quirks is an irrational love of the white carpet that was here when we bought the house. Now, when I say white, I'm talking in terms that are more conceptual than literal. You see, we have two cats, both of whom have holes on each end that con-stantly spew disgusting things over the allegedly white carpet. It's an old rug, so no stain will clean entirely, no matter what technol-ogy is employed. In reality, it's more of a leopard pattern now. Not a healthy leopard either.

This carpet doesn't just allow stains, it *invites* them. If a bum-blebee passes gas anywhere in North America, my carpet gets a little browner in sympathy. This is a dangerous carpet to walk on. In fact, my carpet is the only one specifically mentioned in the international land mine treaty. Once a month I have a team from the United Nations stop by to deactivate as much of it as they can. We've lost a few Spaniards and a Canadian.

Since I am the person who works at home all day, it is my job to handle any new carpet disasters. This occupies much of my waking hours. I spray and I rub and I steam, and then I start over on a new area. Much of my day is spent on my hands and knees dealing with cat-related expectorations. For a change of pace, I clean the litter box.

To me, the obvious solution is to replace the stain-loving white carpet with something made in this century—something that resists stains. The technology exists. That way, the carpet would be easy to clean, and when it was done it would be pleasant to look at.

But Pam likes the "white" carpet. I cannot talk her out of it. So I live like a twelfth-century serf, crawling around in the stench and stains of animal debris. Sometimes I fantasize that one of the king's men will gallop by and lop off my head with a broadsword, thus ending my agony.

Meanwhile my cats are shedding hair like an aging dandelion in a hurricane. I believe Freddie can actually aim and shoot a solid stream of hair, like some sort of cat superhero. He's spraying the love seat with hair as I write this.

The other big problem of being famous is that people want to mail you things that you don't want. Most of these people are well-meaning, so I feel bad complaining. But it's a much bigger problem than you'd ever expect. This was an entirely unanticipated downside of being a semifamous cartoonist.

TYPICAL DAILY CONVERSATION

Kind Stranger: So, I hear you have cats.

Me: Yes.

Kind Stranger: What's your mailing address? I'll send over some poems about cats that I wrote when I was drunk. You'll get a kick out of them.

Me: Um . . .

Kind Stranger: I also know a guy who carves potatoes into animals. I'll ask him to make you some cats. When should I drop them off?

Me: Um . . .

So that's my life. It's mostly about cleaning cat stains and avoiding the kindness of strangers. If that sort of thing appeals to you, then by all means follow the advice in this book and leverage your happiness into money, fame, and success. Just don't say you weren't warned.

Final Postscript

Freddie, the aforementioned cat, passed into cat heaven as I was finishing up this book. He was high-maintenance, but he was my biggest source of workplace joy. I would gladly spend a year cleaning carpet stains for another ten minutes with him.

Freddie taught me a lot about finding joy. For him, a nap on top of my warm computer monitor and a baby's sock stuffed full of catnip were all he needed to have a splendid day. Even in his twilight he never missed a chance to find joy or to give it. His frail body would somehow make it down the stairs and to the door to greet me every time I came home, no matter how many times I went in and out during the day. When he ate, it was with a gusto that seemed as if he were tasting food for the first time in his life. When I brushed him, he purred like a lawn mower. He lived in the moment until the moment was gone.

My final advice—and the only one in this book that won't get you fired, sued, or beaten—is to get a pet if you don't have one. That way, at least one thing will go right for you every day. Your job might still suck, but it will suck less. If you already have a pet, give it a hug right now. You're done with this book. There's no excuse. That, my friends, is joy.